HAUNTED
LIVERPOOL

VOLUME TWO

Published by The Bluecoat Press, Liverpool
Book design by March Graphic Design Studio, Liverpool
Cover illustration by Tim Webster
Printed by Graham & Heslip

ISBN 9781904438724

THE BLUECOAT PRESS
3 Brick Street
Liverpool L1 0BL

Telephone 0151 707 2390
Website www.bluecoatpress.co.uk

Front cover *Night of the Black Rats*, page 51

TOM SLEMEN

HAUNTED LIVERPOOL

VOLUME TWO

THE BLUECOAT PRESS

CONTENTS

INTRODUCTION

The Truth-seekers' battle goes on day and night.
Kabir

As I stated in the introduction to *Haunted Liverpool 1*, science no longer holds any absolute truths. It has even been found to be hopelessly inadequate in explaining such elemental forces as gravity and light. Therefore, how can we expect scientists to unravel the mysteries within this book? With the exception of Edinburgh University, which has a department dedicated to the study of the paranormal, and a couple of universities in the USA, there are no government funded projects in the UK looking into ghosts and other psychic phenomena. Some time ago I wrote to David Canter, Professor of Psychology at Liverpool University, asking why there was no Chair of Parapsychology. The reply I received, written on his behalf, was both amusing and typical:

Dear Tom,
Your query on parapsychology has reached me. You should realise that the Edinburgh Department is the only one of its kind in Europe and, in fact, I only know of one other department, which is in the USA. You should appreciate that the reason very few psychologists are interested in ghosts and the like is because over 100 years of study has shown that although these phenomena tell us something about the person who experiences them, they tell us nothing about the spirit world. So, if at any point you wanted a psychologist to explain what people were experiencing, I am sure we could find one.
All the best, I McIntosh, (pp David Canter)

In other words, people who see ghosts need their heads examining. It is infuriating to think that we are paying taxes so that the government can give a hefty wage packet to myopic people of this sort in their ivory towers. If people who see ghosts are insane, we must include Her Majesty the Queen, who, with her husband, Prince Phillip and Princess Alexandra, has attended many séances and seen her late father, King George VI.

Then there is the famous psychologist, Carl Gustav Jung, the founder of Jungian psychology, who saw a ghostly head resting on a pillow next to his when he was in bed one night. It is also said that US Presidents, Kennedy and Roosevelt, both saw the spectre of President Lincoln on several occasions in the White House. In his fascinating book, *X-Rated: The Paranormal Secrets of the Stars*, author Michael Munn informs us that many showbiz stars have had spooky encounters, including celebrities like Liverpool-born star, Cilla Black, one of the highest-paid entertainers on British television.

Munn explains how Cilla saw the ghost of a teenaged girl, standing by her bed, on several occasions over a period of seven years. When the visitations first happened, Cilla thought that one of her children had come into the room, but when she looked up, she saw what she described as "a sweet-looking young girl standing there, wearing a long old-fashioned dress". Cilla did not feel at all frightened by the apparition, in fact she claimed that she actually liked her being there. She has tried to speak to the ghost on several occasions, but she never looks at her or answers her questions, instead, just smiling and floating away through the door.

Munn also mentions other highly successful celebrities who have seen ghosts or had psychic experiences; people like Madonna, Roger Moore, Telly Savalas, Peter Sellers,

Tommy Steele and Sir Alec Guinness to name but a few. I am sure that most of these celebrities would be very angry if Liverpool University's Mr McIntosh told them that the things they had seen were all in the mind.

It was recently discovered that if you hammer two nails into a stone wall and then wire the nails to the microphone socket of a domestic tape recorder, you can sometimes record mysterious and inexplicable sounds, potentially related to the supernatural. This intriguing experiment has been carried out in buildings where ghostly phenomena have been reported over the years and phantom voices have been recorded. It seems that the stone walls of many residences that are reputedly haunted contain silica, ferric oxide and quartz, which may act as a natural tape recorder.

Ferric oxide is the brown material that cassette tapes are partly made of and it seems to be the main culprit. It is as though, when the stones are slightly compressed, perhaps through temperature changes, the quartz generates what is known as piezo-electricity, which is a way of producing electrical energy by applying pressure to a crystal. When you click some electric lighters, the blue ignition spark is produced by the pressure you have exerted on a small piece of piezo-electric crystal. When this piezo-electricity flows through the stone wall, it powers up the audio recordings in the stone's ferric oxide, producing the sounds. It is an exciting breakthrough and may eventually explain how ghostly sounds become recorded in rock.

In this book I mention several mysterious disappearances, the cause of which may well be supernatural, yet I suspect that they are merely cases of a phenomenon known in the occult world as 'teleportation'.

In the 1950s, the pioneering UFO writer, MK Jessup, unearthed a peculiar story from the archives of Spain's legal records concerning the trial of a Spanish guard, Gil Perez. Perez had allegedly been on duty at the Governor's Palace in Manila on 25 October 1593, when he suddenly found himself in the main square of Mexico City. His dramatic appearance from nowhere naturally alarmed the passers-by and the guard quickly attracted the attention of the Mexican authorities. Perez was unable to explain how he had been transported instantaneously thousands of miles across the globe from the Philippines.

The only details he could supply amounted to vague descriptions and a garbled account of a mysterious cloud, which enveloped him moments before his trip, but he could remember nothing more. Perez stated that the sinister incident had occurred minutes after the assassination of the Manilan Governor and three months later, a ship from the Philippines reached Mexico and confirmed the assassination and other details of the soldier's story. In such a superstitious age, Perez was lucky not to have been burnt at the stake.

However, such was the fate of a man in 1655 who was deemed to be a black magician by the Spanish Inquisition because he was inexplicably transported from the Portuguese colony in Goa, India, to Portugal, in the proverbial twinkling of an eye.

The famed student of the unexplained, Charles Fort (1874-1932) was intrigued by a plethora of reports, gleaned from newspaper cuttings and historical records, of people who had somehow been transferred from one place to another without any physical movement through the usual three dimensions of space. Fort coined the term 'teleportation' to describe this phenomenon, a word which is now only found in the pages of science-fiction. That, of course, does not debase the concept of teleportation. Television, computers, lasers and the atom bomb were also only words in science-fiction literature until not so long ago.

The logic of cybernetics suggests that every physical object can, in principle, be reduced to encoded information which could be transmitted on a carrier wave. This may seem a little far-fetched, but the idea of compressing Beethoven's works on to a compact disc and the technology of a home computer would have seemed equally unbelievable to your Victorian counterpart; it is just a matter of time and technological progress. Today we can send television pictures, radio bulletins and faxes anywhere in the world via satellite; tomorrow we may be able to actually send ourselves in a similar way. But how will such a feat of technology be achieved? There are two areas of science which may provide the breakthrough in teleportation – electronics and theoretical physics.

Electronics is progressing at an alarming rate. In 1948, the invention of the transistor was hailed as a quantum leap in technology and its inventors were awarded the Nobel Prize for their work, but there are now tiny silicon chips, in common use, which contain over 18 million transistors. These chips are becoming more complex each year. Let us imagine a time in the not too distant future when we will have chips that are complex enough to store and process the exact positions of every atom in the human body. There are billions of atoms in your body, but there are mainframe computers in existence that could easily handle the sums involved. Now, if we can envisage a device that could scan the human body atom by atom and store the positions of each atom on our super-computer chips, we are halfway to constructing a teleporter.

Along these lines, a similar body-scanner is routinely used in hospitals and works by the principle of nuclear magnetic resonance. In such hospital scanners, the atoms in the patient's body are mapped by a computer and presented on a screen in a series of cross sections. The problem is, of course, translating the information in our scanner back into atoms, for this formidable task we would need something along the lines of a particle accelerator, which could convert basic atoms of hydrogen (the simplest atom) into the various carbon, nitrogen and other atoms of which we are made.

This hypothetical 'matter transmitter' would also be an advanced duplicating machine, because it would merely copy the original person atom by atom. To be a true teleporter, our machine would have to actually transfer the original subject to a destination and, in theory, this could be achieved by warping the very fabric of space. Two of the greatest geniuses of the twentieth century – Albert Einstein and Professor John A Wheeler (co-inventor of the H-Bomb), have claimed that space can be distorted and bent by gravity and high-density magnetic fields to provide a form of instantaneous transportation across superspace.

According to Wheeler, superspace is another form of space which runs alongside our own, but it does not have time as we know it. As long ago as 1927, Einstein had reached a similar conclusion. That year he completed a paper entitled *Unified Field Theory for Gravitation and Electricity*. Shortly after the theory was published in Germany, the paper was suddenly withdrawn from circulation. In the scientific community there were rumours that Einstein had withdrawn his paper because he thought that his work was too far ahead of its time and feared that the military powers of pre-Nazi Germany would abuse it.

After World War II (and the horrors of Hiroshima and Nagasaki) the pacifist philosopher, Bertrand Russell – a close friend of Einstein – read his secret paper on the Unified Field Theory. Lord Russell enigmatically remarked that mankind was not ready for such a far-reaching theory. Others who have read Einstein's intriguing paper claim that he had formulated ground-breaking equations, showing that magnetism and gravity were related and also how space could be distorted with high-powered magnetic fields in such a way as to provide instant travel to any point on this earth, or away from it.

If Einstein's theory is correct, how would it explain the teleportation of Gil Perez in 1593? No one in those times would have possessed the technology to generate space-warping magnetic fields. Perhaps nature herself may have been the culprit. The source of the earth's magnetic field is still a complete mystery, but satellite surveys of the geomagnetic field have revealed a host of hitherto unknown magnetic storms – localised points on the earth's surface where the earth's magnetic field becomes very intense for a matter of minutes. Most of these storms occur at sea, but some have formed on land and have actually disrupted radio communications.

Perhaps Gil Perez was in the eye of one of these storms in 1593. If so, perhaps the Spanish guard was transported across the world via Professor Wheeler's superspace. The magnetic-storm theory would also explain the disappearances in the Bermuda Triangle, where many of the final radio messages from lost ships and planes mention disorientation because of a spinning magnetic compass.

So much for teleportation; what technology would we use for contacting or detecting ghosts? Have you noticed that no matter how sophisticated an alarm system is today, something always seems to trigger it? Most households nowadays are fitted with basic burglar alarms which are activated when anything moves in the vicinity of their infra-red passive detectors. These alarms are becoming something of a national menace according to statistics from various noise pollution groups, so what is causing them to go off? The answer may well be ghosts.

An excellent example is the case of an alarm that went off at the Butterflies nightclub in Oldham around 1997. Police raced to what they thought was either a break-in or a faulty alarm. When they arrived at the premises, they found no sign of a break-in or anyone in the place. However, when they looked closely at the videotape from the security cameras, they were intrigued to see the shape of a youth in a white t-shirt walking down a corridor. The figure appeared to be semi-transparent. It even seemed to pass straight through a closed locked door, when the alarm went off. The owners of the club believe that the spectre is the ghost of an electrician who was fatally electrocuted during a rewiring job at the club many years ago.

Such cases seem to indicate that ghosts can trigger infra-red alarms, but could there be some other way we can detect them? I believe the answer lies in the plant kingdom. This idea will probably be ridiculed, but here goes. In February 1965, Cleve Baxter, a former CIA employee and one of the leading experts in lie-detection, discovered that if he connected his polygraph (lie detector) electrodes to the leaves of one of his houseplants and watered it, the trace on his pen recorder did not record an increase in the electrical conductivity of the plant. This amazed him, because it seemed to run against the basic laws of electrical resistance.

The trace on his machine instead showed a pattern of steadily decreasing conductivity, which seemed to indicate that the plant was undergoing a relaxing experience when it was watered. This finding encouraged Baxter to conduct further experiments with the plant. When he merely thought about burning a leaf of the wired-up plant with his lighter, the pen of the polygraph recorder made a sharp upward jump. To Baxter, there seemed to be only one possible but incredible explanation – the plant was somehow reading his mind!

To discount the possibility that his polygraph was faulty, or that the plant reaction was some kind of anomaly, he also tested hundreds of other plants, using many different models of polygraphs; the results were always the same, the plants seemed to possess some sort of consciousness. There is still experimental work being carried out on Baxter's findings, but scientists are unable to agree on how, or why, plants exhibit psycho-galvanic readings when they are wired up. It is now known, and widely accepted, however, that plants certainly are able to respond to certain kinds of music and human speech.

An excellent example is the renowned nurseryman Luther Burbank, of Santa Rosa, California, who spent many years at the turn of the century developing a new variety of spineless cactus. When botanists asked him how he had managed to produce such a species of plant, Burbank calmly replied that he talked them. "I say to them, 'you have nothing to fear. You don't need your defensive thorns. I will protect you'," was Burbank's controversial reply.

Another botany expert who has proved that plants are capable of directly responding to stimuli is Jagadis Chandra Bose, the professor of physics at Presidency College, Calcutta. Bose built a device to amplify the microscopic movement of plant tissue. He discovered that plants feel pain, as well as also exhibiting emotional responses as complex as those of a human being. In 1917 Bose was knighted for his work and in 1920 he was made a Fellow of the Royal Society. Later in the 1960s, several experimenters at the University of Ottawa showed that seedlings exposed to sound, grew more quickly when the sound was high-pitched. In the experiment, African Violets were placed next to the loudspeakers of a hi-fi system and it was found that they tended to lean away from the speaker if the music being played was rock 'n' roll, but the music of Haydn, Bach and sitar musicians made them lean towards the speaker and also to grow faster. You can easily try this simple experiment out on your own plants!

If plants are as highly sensitive as Baxter and the other far-sighted botanists are suggesting, they would make ideal sensors if they were wired to a polygraph and placed within a haunted dwelling. Perhaps any psychic activity that is not perceptible to us could be detected by the plants. It is just an idea. Anyway, do read on and enjoy the following stories from my cabinet of curiosities.

BRUNEL'S JINXED SUPERSHIP

Mariners are renowned for their superstitions. To the seafarer, the sight of an albatross over a ship is a warning of an approaching storm and, as Coleridge recounted in *The Rime of the Ancient Mariner*, to kill such a bird would bring an eternity of bad luck.

Even today there are fishermen who will stay ashore if they happen to meet a priest or a nun on the way to join their ship. There are still some old seadogs who will refuse to set foot on board a ship which has had its name changed, a superstition that is said to date back to 1867, when a Nova Scotian brigantine called the *Amazon* was renamed the *Marie Celeste*. The rechristened ship suffered a catalogue of calamities and was finally found abandoned, drifting near the Azores in 1872. To this day, no one knows what became of her crew.

Sailors are also extremely wary about unlucky cargoes. When an allegedly ominous mummy of the Ancient Egyptian princess, Ammon-Ra, was transferred from the British Museum into the hold of a famous liner in April 1912, many seamen were convinced that their vessel would be jinxed. It may have been sheer coincidence, but the same liner sank on her maiden voyage. She was the *Titanic*.

Another ship which had an unlucky maiden voyage was the 2,000-ton steel bark *Hinemoa*. During her voyage of 1892, four apprentice seamen died of typhoid. Then the captain later went insane. The second captain of the bark turned into a ruthless thief and ended up in prison, the third became an alcoholic, the fourth died of natural causes in his cabin and the fifth committed suicide by blowing his brains out. The sixth captain of the *Hinemoa* survived the jinxed ship but, under his command, the vessel capsized and two sailors were swept to their deaths when the ship eventually righted itself. Finally, in 1908, the ship became a write-off when she drifted ashore on the west cost of Scotland. An engineer who worked on the ship firmly believed that it had been jinxed as a result of using tons of soil from an East London graveyard as ballast.

Without a doubt, the unluckiest ship that ever sailed was built at the yards of John Scott Russell in Milwall, London, over a period of three years in the late 1850s. The *Great Eastern* was the brainchild of one of the greatest engineers of all time; Isambard Kingdom Brunel. At 19,000 tons, the gigantic vessel was the most ambitious engineering project of the nineteenth century. The colossal 692-foot long, iron-plated, double hull of Brunel's supership surpassed the dimensions of Noah's fabled Ark and she was capable of carrying 4,000 passengers.

The ship which the maritime world called the 'Wonder of the Seas' sported an unheard-of six masts and traditional maritime nomenclature could not be applied to them, so they were referred to as Monday, Tuesday, Wednesday, Thursday, Friday and Saturday. Motive power was to be supplied by a 24-foot, steam-driven propeller, or gigantic paddle wheels and, should her steam engines fail, the ship would simply unfurl her gargantuan sails. The Herculean vessel could also stockpile enough coal to provide a journey from England to Australia and back without the need to refuel.

While the *Great Eastern* was under construction at Milwall, two hundred rivet gangs worked on the ship's novel double hull, until a staggering three million rivets had been firmly hammered into place. The outer hull was separated from the inner one by a gap of three feet. Within the hulls there was an innovative arrangement of 16 watertight bulkheads, designed to make the ship virtually unsinkable.

One day in January 1857, during the round-the-clock racket of hammering and banging, somebody noticed that one of the riveters and his apprentice were missing. The weeks passed by, but the two missing men were nowhere to be found. Another riveter, an Irishman, reported that he had heard a strange pounding noise coming from within the double hull, but no one took him seriously and he was ignored and the noises were never investigated.

The width of the River Thames at the Millwall shipyards was too narrow to allow the *Great Eastern* to be launched lengthways, so the ship had to be ushered into the river sideways; an operation that took an agonising three months, during which all kinds of technical difficulties were experienced. During this protracted procedure, Brunel became ill through overwork and worry. He was only 53 years old but looked at least 20 years older, through working for years without adequate sleep. He opened the Times newspaper one day to read, with bitterness, that the editor had dismissed his time-consuming project as a white elephant:

'There she lies on the very brink of the noble river which is to carry her to the ocean, but she will not wet her lips.'

However, the leviathan finally did 'wet her lips' on 31 January 1858, after being eased 330 feet down a slipway by buckling hydraulic jacks. Brunel himself remarked that, "Putting St Paul's to sea would have been easier!"

On the very day which the *Great Eastern* was launched, Brunel was standing on deck, unable to believe that his magnificent creation was finally about to be in service, when he suffered a massive stroke and collapsed. He remained gravely ill for the next year and a half and, on 15 September 1859, he died after hearing that a steam pipe had burst on the *Great Eastern* during her trial run to Weymouth. The massive explosion had destroyed a funnel and the searing cloud of escaping steam had boiled five stokers to death.

In a separate tragedy, at around the same time, another crewman had fallen on to a paddle wheel and been instantly smashed to pieces. Three members of the ship's crew had talked of hearing pounding noises within the hull just before the two tragedies took place.

The astronomical costs of the delayed launch – over £1 million – brought financial ruin to the Eastern Navigation Company, who had planned to employ Brunel's ship on long voyages to India and Australia. The Great Ship Company took over the project and opted instead for the quick profits of the North Atlantic run. From that point on, the unlucky career of the *Great Eastern* started in earnest. The first planned voyage to the United States in 1861 had to be cancelled because the repair work to the ship's damaged funnel and boiler took longer than expected.

The frustrated directors of the Great Ship Company were eager to get some return on their troublesome investment, so, as an interim measure, they moved the *Great Eastern* to Holyhead in Wales, to put her on display to paying sightseers. But, shortly after arriving at Holyhead, one of the fiercest gales in living memory tore in from the Irish Sea and ripped the mighty vessel from her moorings.

For 18 agonising hours she was tossed about in the coastal waters, but she rode the storm well, while other ships sank all around her, thanks to her new-fangled double hull and waterproofed bulkheads. After the gale had moved away, the *Great Eastern* was an awesome sight, as she steamed majestically from the storm-clouded horizon, back to Holyhead. However, she did not escape unscathed, as the storm had caused thousands of pounds worth of damage to the ship's grand saloon.

Three months later, the *Great Eastern's* first captain, William Harrison, the coxswain, along with the nine-year-old son of the chief purser were all drowned, when a sudden violent storm swamped their gig as they were going ashore. In the seafaring world, nothing casts a darker shadow over a ship's character than the death of a captain prior to a maiden voyage. So, when the news of the three deaths reached London, the directors of the Great Ship Company resigned immediately.

The new board of directors, eager to restore the public's confidence in the seemingly jinxed ship, announced that the *Great Eastern* would leave Southampton for New York on 9 June 1860. The voyage was a financial disaster. All the adverse publicity had earned Brunel's ship a bad reputation and people opted for the smaller, more reliable, Cunard ships. Hundreds of tickets for the *Great Eastern's* maiden voyage were printed, but when the 9 June arrived, the ship still was not ready because of technical difficulties with its engine.

Finally, on 16 June, a mere 35 passengers boarded the

mammoth vessel. The new captain, who had never made an Atlantic crossing before, commanded a crew of 418. During the 12-day crossing, poor quality, economy coal caused thick, carbonaceous deposits to form on the linings of the funnel casings, which caused the engines to overheat and this, in turn, caused the main dining room area to become intolerably hot.

Despite all these problems, when the *Great Eastern* arrived in New York, she was greeted by thousands of cheering sightseers. But things soon turned sour again when some of these onlookers attempted to go on board the British ship and they were promptly told that they would have to pay a one dollar admission fee for the privilege. People who had been forced to pay the fee were determined to get their money's worth and they pocketed anything on the ship that was not bolted down for souvenirs.

It was announced that the ship was to make a two-day excursion and 2000 people were soon queueing for tickets. But the two-day outing turned into a nightmare when it was learned that only 300 beds were available. As a result of this, over a thousand passengers had to sleep on the deck, where cinders and a steady drizzle of soot from the damaged funnels rained down on them all through the night. To make matters even worse, a pipe burst in the ship's storage room, soaking the food supplies. The only foods that were salvaged were dried chicken, over-salted meat and stale biscuits and even for these unsavoury items, the passengers were charged exorbitant prices.

By the time the burst pipe had been fixed, all the ship's drinking water had leaked away. The infuriated passengers looked forward to a speedy landing, but even that failed to be straightforward; through some unaccountable navigational error, the *Great Eastern* had drifted way off course during the night and was over one hundred miles out to sea by dawn. When the ship finally reached New York, the hungry, dirty and weary passengers scrambled to disembark. Not surprisingly, when a second excursion was announced, only a handful of tickets were purchased.

New Yorkers were sorely disappointed with the steam ship, so she returned to England and even this trip was plagued by misfortune. The screw shaft gave out in mid-Atlantic and, at Milford Haven, the ship fouled the rope of a small boat and drowned two of its passengers. Hours after the tragedy, the *Great Eastern* smashed into the frigate *Blenheim*, seriously damaging the latter's hull.

In September 1861, the unfortunate liner was struck by a hurricane in mid-Atlantic. Both side paddles were ripped off by the storm, which also tore the lifeboats away from the deck and unhinged the enormous rudder. The repairs cost over £60,000. In the following year, the *Great Eastern* was steaming through Long Island Sound near New York Harbour, when the ship struck an uncharted rock, which created a gash, 83 feet long and 9 feet wide, in the outer hull. The repairs this time cost in excess of £70,000.

The ill-starred liner was put up for auction in 1864 and was bought for a mere £25,000. Her buyers put her to work as a cable layer, but bad luck still bedevilled the vessel. In 1869, she steamed from Ireland to Newfoundland, laying a telegraph cable on the seabed as she sailed, but when she was 1,186 miles out into the Atlantic, a minor accident caused the cable to snap. The severed end sank three miles to the ocean bed and all attempts to retrieve it failed.

Further commercial missions were also dogged by one disaster after another and so the ship was eventually brought back to Milford Haven and literally abandoned by her owners. For 12 years the *Great Eastern* was left to rust. By

1886, it was decided that the derelict ship (whose hull was, by this time, covered with a layer of barnacles six feet deep) was nothing but an obstacle to the shipping lines, so the dilapidated hulk was brought to Liverpool, where she was anchored in the Mersey, emblazoned with advertising signs. Brunel must have turned in his grave when his 'wonder of the seas' was exploited and cheapened in this way.

The *Great Eastern* was sold by auction by Messrs Dixon and Moore – two Liverpool businessmen – to a firm of metal dealers. Even during her final voyage to a scrapyard near Birkenhead, she was involved in a collision with a tug in the Mersey, which subsequently almost sank after sustaining heavy damage.

It was no easy task to break up the reinforced double hull of the ship, so the wreckers' iron ball was invented for the task. Three days into the formidable demolition job, the wreckers' ball smashed into the hull, dislodging a large plate. When the ball impacted into the ship again, something was seen to fall from a hole in the hull. Two demolition experts gave orders to cease work and went to investigate the object which had fallen out of the ship on to the piles of scrap at the quayside.

They were shocked to find that it was the skeleton of a man, draped in musky clothes. Another skeleton – that of a much younger male – was later found in another compartment, sandwiched between the two hulls. The skeletons were later formally identified as those of the missing riveter and his apprentice by members of their families who had travelled from Canning Town and Dagenham. Many believed that the chilling discovery explained the *Great Eastern's* jinxed history.

The Marie Celeste Connection

Most unsolved mystery buffs are familiar with the basic outline of the story of the *Marie Celeste*. She left New York in November 1872 under the command of Captain Briggs with 1,700 barrels of crude alcohol in her hold, bound for Genoa in Italy. On board were Briggs' wife and two-year-old daughter and a crew of eight men.

Almost a month later, David Moorhouse, captain of a ship called the *Dei Gratia*, caught sight of a speck on the horizon, 500 miles east of the Azores. When he scrutinised it more closely through his telescope, he saw that it was a ship that was sailing erratically. He dispatched a boarding party over to investigate and they found the ship, the *Marie Celeste*, totally deserted. The only lifeboat was missing but, in all other respects, the ship was completely seaworthy.

There was a full six months' supply of food and water on the ship and also the crew's oilskins, boots, pipes and tobacco had all been left behind. It was obvious that everyone on board had left the ship in a tremendous hurry for some unknown reason. After an extensive search, it was discovered that only the navigation instruments appeared to have been taken.

Further investigation revealed that someone had struck the ship's rail with an axe and, in the cargo hold, one of the barrels had been opened. The captain's sword was found on his bed in his cabin and, on a slate, someone had chalked the words, 'Fanny, my dear wife, Frances M R'.

Captain Moorhouse towed the derelict ship to Gibraltar and, after a lengthy court of enquiry, he was awarded a salvage cheque for the princely sum of £2000 for his troubles.

No one has ever fully solved the mystery of the *Marie*

Celeste but quite a few people later came forward, claiming that they were survivors of the sea's most famous mystery. Most of these claimants were either publicity-seekers or just plain conmen, out to make a quick buck. But, curiously, two Liverpool sailors were amongst those who said they had been on board the *Marie Celeste* during her fateful last voyage.

One of these was a ninety-two-year-old cook from Maryland Street named Lawrence Keating. He claimed that he had joined the crew at the last minute when one of the original sailors on the *Marie Celeste* refused to set sail because he believed in the ancient superstition that it was unlucky to embark on a merchant voyage with a woman on board (in this case the captain's wife). Keating's account detailed how the ship ran into a hurricane in the mid-Atlantic, which almost turned the ship on its end. During the storm, the piano on board came loose from its moorings and crushed the captain's wife and the captain was utterly devastated by his terrible loss.

Adamantly refusing to confine his wife's decomposing body into the sea, he placed her in the only lifeboat and towed it by rope, behind the *Marie Celeste*. This action caused deep consternation amongst the crew and somebody eventually severed the rope and a fight resulted. The captain then went on the rampage, wielding an axe and threatening everyone in sight. After killing most of the crew, with the storm still raging, he was washed into the sea. Keating had allegedly survived the whole incident by hiding in the cargo hold. However, no one believed his bizarre story and he died two months after his revelations, so his account could be neither authenticated, nor dismissed.

Another Scouser, William Foyle, a notorious thief and confidence-trickster, literally leapt aboard a ship named the

City of Ragusa bound for Boston, in 1870. Billy Foyle was an inventive and imaginative conman, who was in the habit of selling fake maps of South African diamond mines to the gullible public. When he arrived in America, he embarked on a further series of frauds and, eventually, when the American authorities began to close in on his illegal, entrepreneurial activities, in order to evade capture, he allegedly stowed away on a brig – the *Marie Celeste*.

Now, Billy Foyle had gained such a well-deserved reputation from telling so many whoppers, that no one attempted to believe his version of the *Marie Celeste* mystery, when he reached Liverpool in 1873. At a waterfront tavern in Paradise Street, he told a motley crew of associates that he had been woken up in the hold of the *Marie Celeste* to the sound of an ominous, deafening rumble. Apparently, it was caused by the alcohol in the barrels, fermenting in the sweltering tropical heat.

He was convinced that an explosion was imminent, so he was forced to break his cover and scramble hurriedly up on deck. To his total bewilderment, there was no one there. All the crew had abandoned ship and were huddled together in the only lifeboat, which was attached to the ship by a long line of around 300 yards. Foyle quickly realised that they had also been frightened of the unstable cargo and had consequently put as much distance between themselves and the ship as possible, by taking refuge in the lifeboat.

Foyle repeatedly pleaded with them to allow him on to the boat, but they refused, so he angrily grabbed an axe and severed the tow rope. The lifeboat carrying the crew drifted off towards the horizon and Foyle fell to his knees and prayed for salvation. Inexplicably, the cargo gradually stabilised and the danger subsided. When Captain Moorhouse, who found the ship, was towing the *Marie*

Celeste into the harbour at Gibraltar, he saw Foyle come out on deck. Potentially, he could have ruined the salvage prize, so Moorhouse let him go. This account all ties in with the established facts. At the court of enquiry, witnesses stated that an unaccounted-for crew member left the *Dei Gratia* and set out for England. Mystery solved?

I recently uncovered an article in an old newspaper which may throw some light on the fate of the *Marie Celeste's* crew. On 16 May 1873, the *Daily Albion* of Liverpool reported that fishermen at Baudus, in Asturias, near Madrid, had spotted two rafts floating in the Atlantic coastal waters off the Spanish mainland. One of the rafts had a corpse lashed to its side and was flying an American flag. The second raft carried five decomposing bodies. For some unaccountable reason, the reports were never fully looked into, so we will never know from which ship the dead bodies originated. Could they possibly have been from the *Marie Celeste?*

CARBON COPY

Me and my shadow, walking down the avenue ...
Billy Rose

We often say, when impossible demands are made of us, that we cannot be in two places at once, as if we are stating the obvious. Yet there have been many recorded instances of the doppelganger – an exact double of a living person that is supposed, by legend, to stalk us all. These phantasms of the living are said to stay out of sight of their worldly counterpart until he or she is approaching death, or experiencing a serious illness; then they usually visit their twin, or even their double's friends. Here is an intriguing report of a doppelganger incident which is alleged to have taken place in Everton in May 1995.

Terry saw his own doppelganger three times and, on each occasion, he was terrified by the experience. When he encountered it the first time he was on a bus up in Walton Road. He glanced out of the window and saw his spitting image, dressed in the very same clothes he was wearing himself that day, coming out of a newsagents, reading a copy of the *Daily Mirror*, Terry's favourite tabloid newspaper.

Terry often visited that particular newsagents shop to purchase his newspapers and magazines and was extremely shaken by the sighting. He stood up on the bus and rushed to the rear window of the vehicle to get a better glimpse of his eerie carbon copy, almost knocking an old lady to the ground in the process.

On the second occasion, Terry walked into his local barber's and took a seat, to wait his turn. The barber glanced round and commented to Terry that his hair had grown very fast. Terry just grinned amicably, without appreciating what he actually meant. When the barber had finished with his customer, he walked over to Terry, eyed his hair with a puzzled look and muttered, "You were only in here last week."

"No, I wasn't," Terry protested, thinking the hairdresser was confusing him with someone else.

"Yes you were. Don't you remember? You were feeling a bit depressed," the barber insisted.

"I never set foot in here last ..." Terry began, when he suddenly remembered the doppelganger incident on the bus. He related the incident to the barber, who turned white and started talking to Terry's mirror image, a common idiosyncrasy of many hairdressers.

"You're winding me up," he said.

"Before God, I saw my double," continued Terry, who

was a born-again Christian. "Same clothes, same height and build, same face."

"You're giving me the creeps, Tel," the hairdresser said with a shudder, still addressing his mirror image.

"You said he was depressed. What did you mean?" Terry continued.

"That's just it, You – or he, never said anything, which wasn't like you. You usually can't stop nattering, can you? I presumed you were down in the dumps. Oh, I think you're having me on."

The barber smiled at Terry, expecting him to admit to some hoax, but it was plain that he was genuinely worried.

Later that day, Terry visited an acquaintance of his who did the Tarot cards and was really into the occult. He told Terry that he was being stalked by his doppelganger, which meant that his number was up. "This is brilliant. I'd love to see it. When you meet your doppelganger and touch it, you both die, like matter touching anti-matter, it's mutual destruction," he added insensitively.

Feeling completely distraught by this stage, Terry told her about the double and it was she who wrote a letter on his behalf and addressed it to me at Radio Merseyside. I receive a considerable amount of mail from time-wasters, attention seekers and various other cranks so, initially, I concluded that someone in listener-land was playing a prank on me but, eventually, I rang Terry's neighbour and arranged a meeting. Terry was very sincere and asked me to refrain from turning his bizarre predicament into fodder for the media. He did not want his name or address to be given on air, although I assured him he would be able to come on the *Billy Butler Show* without supplying his name.

"Billy and Wally are very understanding in these matters," I told him, "and they wouldn't treat this unusual situation in their usual jokey, sarcastic manner, if they thought it would upset you."

Alas, Terry refused to come on air. He asked me to tell him frankly if I also thought his number was up. I explained to him that I have read an awful lot of literature on doppelgangers over the years which dispelled the myth that they were an omen of impending doom. It was just an old wives' tale and nothing more and I told him so. I advised him to carry a camera so that he could take a snapshot of his double, just to prove to himself that it was not all in his mind. However, he seemed insulted by the suggestion and testily stated that he did not need to prove that his double was real, he just wanted to be rid of it. In the end, I told a psychical researcher in Hunts Cross about the case and he looked into it.

He became like another shadow, tailing Terry everywhere he went. He, too, saw the doppelganger, strolling down Barlow Lane one Sunday morning. The lane was deathly quiet and the researcher cried out to Terry, "There it is. It's coming this way." And so it was. The uncanny figure was walking towards the two men, glancing down at the ground, apparently in a sombre mood. Terry turned and was about to flee, as his nerves got the better of him, but the researcher seized him firmly by the shoulders and held him so that he was forced to face his sinister mirror image. When the doppelganger was around fifty feet away, it suddenly noticed its original counterpart and turned and ran, with the researcher running close behind. The doppelganger turned the corner into Westminster Road and when the researcher turned the same corner, seconds later, it had mysteriously vanished.

It was seen on one more occasion, strolling amongst the milling crowds in Church Street, near the entrance to the C&A clothing store, when Terry was in town shopping with his girlfriend. He pointed the double out to her and she was amazed to find that all Terry's accounts of his encounters with his doppelganger were true after all. However, she believed there must be a rational explanation – speculating that perhaps Terry's mother had given birth to twins, who had been separated for some reason. The doppelganger walked up the street and turned a corner with Terry and his girlfriend in hot pursuit, but they lost sight of it in the crowds near the Bluecoat Chambers.

Since that day, Terry has never set eyes on his second self, but a fortnight after the grand finale, there was one last calling card from his alter ego. Terry visited Anfield Cemetery in order to place a bouquet of roses on his mother's grave, but was perplexed to find that someone had already been and placed a similar bouquet. The note attached to the floral tribute read: 'Still miss you loads, Mum. Love, Terry. xxx '

At this Terry snapped. He became paranoid and suspected that his occult-obsessed friend had played a sick joke on him. Later that day he waylaid his friend as he was reading a dusty old tome about the supernatural in his usual haunt – a secondhand bookshop in Mount Pleasant. His friend denied playing any distasteful prank and was quite offended by the suggestion. He even produced a creased rail ticket to prove that he had been staying with his cousin in Wales for the previous three days.

Terry apologised. He was so shaken by his skirmishes with his creepy simulacrum, that he finally moved house and rented a flat near Rodney Street. To date, he has not bumped into his flesh and blood replica. But every time he turns a corner, he wonders if he will see it again.

* * *

Another doppelganger case occurred in the mid-1980s, in a house on Church Road, Wavertree, not a stone's throw from Penny Lane. The four-bedroomed house had no history of hauntings or ghostly goings-on, so it was a shock for the Davis family, and their year-old Labrador, Cecil, to see the phantom of a middle-aged woman walking down their stairs one afternoon. Cecil was so terrified, that he crashed headlong through the bottom pane of glass in the kitchen door in his retreat from the unwelcome entity. Miraculously, he did not even suffer a scratch.

Upon reaching the bottom of the stairs, the ectoplasmic woman seemed to break up into millions of spots before disappearing completely. Mr Davis described how she had dematerialised in the same that Captain Kirk did on *Star Trek* when they beam him up. He said that her image seemed to break up into a myriad of luminous specks. The ghost was seen many more times, mostly during the daytime. It strolled across the front garden lawn on one occasion and was seen by the postman, who initially took it to be a real person, until it performed its usual uncanny dissolving act.

A year later, Mr Davis had an opportunity to work in Hoylake and decided to put his house on the market and move across the water. Imagine his surprise when he met the first person who came to view it – a woman who was identical to the now-familiar phantom lady. Her face, hairstyle and build, were all identical to the apparition's. The woman gave her name as Mrs O'Rourke and she claimed to have been born in the Davis's house in the 1930s and had spent most of her teenage life there. Mr Davis was flabbergasted.

Mrs O'Rourke said that she often visited the house in her mind's eye and imagined walking around its interior. When she had seen the for sale sign outside, she just had to take the opportunity to stop by and view her childhood home. Mr Davis told her about the ghost that had been haunting the house and suggested that it was perhaps her mother's spectre. She gave a lop-sided grin then calmly said: "Oh, no, that wasn't mother. It was probably me. You may think I'm mad, but I think I somehow projected my image here during my nostalgic ramblings. People have told me about this type of thing before. When I couldn't make it to Oxford Street Maternity hospital when my daughter was giving birth because I had the flu, two nurses swore they saw me in the ward where my daughter was."

Mr Davis introduced Mrs O'Rourke to the rest of his family and they were amazed at the likeness between their guest and the resident ghost. When Cecil the dog set eyes on Mrs O'Rourke, he fled for cover beneath the stairs and howled inconsolably. His behaviour seemed to prove that something strange was going on.

Sadly, three months later, Mrs O'Rourke died after a short illness and the Davis family finally sold their house and moved away. As far as I know, the new owners of the house on Church Road have not had any encounters with the phantom lady.

* * *

Yet another doppelganger story, with a Liverpool connection, is mentioned in the July 1991 edition of the *Fortean Times*, a monthly magazine about strange phenomena which derives its name from the iconoclastic philosopher and student of the unexplained, Charles Fort (1874-1932). In the letters column of the magazine, there is an intriguing account of a doppelganger in the north of Liverpool from Rob Gandy of Bebington, on the Wirral.

"About two years ago (1981), I was driving down County Road in Kirkdale, Liverpool, towards the city centre. The traffic was fairly heavy as people were returning home in the early evening. I pulled up at the Spellow Lane traffic lights which were on red – I was about four cars back from the lights in the outside lane. I noticed a rather plump woman, in a garish outfit, cutting through the stationary cars to cross the road. She walked immediately in front of my car, from left to right, before crossing when there was a gap in the oncoming traffic. With her blonde hair piled up on the top of her head and her striking attire, this middle-aged woman was very remarkable in appearance, arguably for the wrong reasons.
The lights changed and I set off down Walton Road into Kirkdale Road, with the traffic flowing reasonably quickly. I then had to stop at the traffic lights at the junction of Great Homer Street – which are about three-quarters of a mile from Spellow Lane. To my amazement, the same woman cut through the stationary vehicles, immediately in front of my car, from left to right. There was no mistaking her, unless she had a twin sister who was dressed identically. There is no way that I can conceive of how the woman managed to travel from the first position to the second, in what must have been about 90 seconds, given the absence of any transport."

All we can do is hazard a guess and presume that all the previous accounts outlined in this chapter are examples of the doppelganger. According to psychical researchers, ghosts of the living are the commonest type of apparition. This claim is backed up by a report carried out in November 1994 by the British Journal of Psychiatry, which examined fifty-six doppelganger episodes that year, including the case of a pilot who saw himself several yards away for a full ten minutes. The report also investigated an intriguing incident concerning a real-looking doppelganger which stalked a retired doctor.

Until scientists can open their minds to the reality of the doppelganger, societies will continue to live in fear of this phenomenon. Perhaps one day we will discover a complex biological mechanism which causes the human body to create a seemingly physical simulacrum of itself. This is not as far-fetched as it seems. Cell multiplication was not discovered until 1844, when the Swiss anatomist and embryologist, Kolliker, astounded the medical world by proving that a human being begins its life as two cells which split up and multiply. Perhaps, when we die, we also split up and produce an intangible etheric body which leaves its earthly replica behind to decay. Maybe in times of illness, or great emotional stress, or in a near death situation, this 'secondary body' is projected from its physical duplicate, or becomes prematurely detached in some way. This theory would make some sense of the doppelganger phenomenon.

A WOMAN'S INTUITION

According to American psychical researchers, most people receive premonitions in their subconscious minds when they are asleep. Experts in the paranormal now believe that, if you keep a notepad by your bed and jot down an account of each dream as soon as you wake up, you will be surprised at how many of the events portrayed in your dreams come to pass over a period of weeks and months, or even days. This theory would explain the baffling phenomenon of déjà vu – the strange sensation people sometimes get which makes them feel that they have already been to a place they have not actually visited before, or know what is going to happen before it occurs. Perhaps you dreamed of being in a particular place months before, but the memory became lost in your subconscious. So keep a dream diary if you want a glimpse of the future – why should it not be ours to see?

In 1838, a German-born businessman named Johann Adolphus kissed his young wife Louisa goodbye, before leaving his palatial house in Abercromby Square. He stepped into a waiting carriage loaded with luggage and waved one last time to her, as she stood tearfully on the front step. The carriage took Mr Adolphus to the docks, where he boarded a steamer bound for Bombay. Johann was an importer of tea and various commodities from India and his stay overseas was likely to last up to six months, maybe more. These bouts of prolonged absence were not exactly conducive to his marriage to Louisa, who was twenty-five years younger than fifty-year-old Johann.

Two months later, Louisa's elderly maidservant and companion, Mrs Hastings, suffered a stroke and died and Louisa's Aunt, Moira Hennessey thought that a sixteen-year-old orphan girl she had adopted would make a fine trainee maid. The young girl was Rose Fitzpatrick, a shy but beautiful brunette who spoke with a slight speech impediment. Louisa hired Rose straight away and found her to be a most conscientious and hardworking girl. One of Louisa's faults was her aloofness where servants and maids were concerned, but she felt as if she had known Rose all her life and the two grew extremely close.

One day, Louisa was watching the new maid cleaning the silverware in the drawing room, when Rose suddenly stopped polishing and began to stare into space, as if in an hypnotic trance.

"What is the matter?" Mrs Adolphus asked, but she received no reply.

After blankly staring for a few moments longer, Rose suddenly announced, with a dazed look, "Mrs Waln has just died ma'am."

"Who is Mrs Waln?" Mrs Adolphus asked, intrigued.

"She was a friend of my guardian, Mrs Hennessey," the young maid explained, with a grave expression.

Nothing more was said until later in the evening, when Moira Hennessey arrived at the house. She unwittingly confirmed Rose's claim; Mrs Hannah Waln, a neighbour of Moira's, had died earlier that day, aged one hundred and two. Strangely enough, she had passed away at the very hour of Rose's bizarre remark. Louisa put the eerie incident down to coincidence, but there were many more unusual episodes concerning the young maid.

One Sunday afternoon, Louisa and Rose were strolling through Abercromby Square on their way to chapel, when a tall man tipped his hat as he walked by. After a few moments, Rose told her employer that the same man had recently written love-letters to her lonely mistress, and added that the gentleman's name was Ralph. Mrs Adolphus was outraged by Rose's bizarre insinuation of a romantic attachment, yet she was intrigued by her supernatural knowledge, because she did indeed know that the man's name was Ralph Foster. He was a business associate of her husband's and had been a guest at her home on two occasions, but had never showed an iota of romantic interest in Louisa, or so she thought …

On the following day, Mrs Adolphus received an anonymous letter from someone who professed to be deeply in love with her. Rose was immediately quizzed about her clairvoyant talent, but the maid said she knew nothing about her strange abilities, only that she had possessed them for as long as she could remember. No further reference was made to the issue for some time, until Louisa's curiosity got the better of her. One quiet evening Mrs Adolphus asked Rose if she could tell her how her husband was keeping, far away in Bombay. The maid sat gazing at the hearth, her eyes fixed on the flames. She then made a very controversial claim which shocked Louisa to the core. She stated that Johann Adolphus had another wife, a Dutch woman named Julia, who was living with him in India. Mrs Adolphus angrily rejected Rose's scandalous assertions at first, but after some months had passed, she ended up travelling to Bombay with a relative to visit her husband, and also to find out whether or not he was a bigamist.

It turned out that he was. Johann had been married to a Julia von Veltheim for four years, leading a double life with a new family in Bombay. On discovering the truth, Louisa ensured that her marriage to him was immediately annulled. Johann remained abroad to avoid imprisonment, while Louisa returned home, her life in tatters. Nevertheless, she retained Johann's properties in Liverpool and slowly began to rebuild her life. Some years later she became engaged to Ralph Foster and in 1842 they married, with Rose as the chief bridesmaid.

DREAMS OF MURDER

On the stormy night of 9 December 1913, fifty-year-old May Shambrook from Anfield went to bed just after twelve o'clock. She was exhausted and so, as soon as her head hit the pillow, she was asleep and was soon experiencing a pleasant dream about a young man who lived across the road in Windermere Street. The man she dreamt about was twenty-one-year-old George Sumner and in the dream, he was smiling at a woman across a room as he swept the floor with a broom. The woman in the dream was beautiful and looked to be about thirty-five to forty years of age. She was smiling back at George as she counted coins on a shop counter of some sort, possibly in a chandler's.

As the vivid dream progressed, George Sumner suddenly flung down the broom and his face became contorted into an extreme expression of pure hatred which was fixed on the woman counting the coins. Her eyes widened in surprise as Sumner lunged at her, grabbing at her breasts and violently ripping off her clothes, before pinning her down on the counter. After raping her, he picked up a wooden stick of some sort and began to batter his petrified victim, who, half naked, was desperately trying to scramble away. The nightmare was so vivid that May Shambrook could see the blood showering Sumner as he hit the woman. The walls of the shop were stippled in crimson blood.

At this point, Mrs Shambrook woke up sweating, and consumed with anxiety. Distraught, she woke her husband and told him about the dream. Still feeling uncomfortable, despite his reassurances, she eventually drifted back to sleep, only to experience another disturbing dream. This time, she could still see the shop of horrors, where she could picture two figures struggling with the corpse of a half-naked woman. The men were doubling the body up and trying to force it into a sack. One of the men was again George Sumner and he was swearing at the corpse because he was having difficulty stuffing it into the sack. The limp head fell sideways confirming that it was the face of the murdered woman from the shop. May woke up even more traumatised. Telling herself to ignore the horrible dream, she lay back, her pulse still racing and hardly slept again that night.

The next day she told a neighbour about the nightmare and she had dismissed it, chortling, "George Sumner wouldn't hurt a fly." Yet on the following day, the local news announced that the manageress of a shop in Old Hall Street had gone missing – the same shop where George Sumner worked. The missing woman was forty-year-old Christina Bradfield, Sumner's boss. A day after the disappearance, Miss Bradfield's body was found floating in the Leeds-Liverpool canal, crumpled awkwardly inside a sack. She was topless, with numerous injuries to her battered head. It also transpired that she had been raped.

After putting together the facts of the case and quizzing the shop staff, the police called at the house of George Sumner, who was suspiciously not at home. His workmate, eighteen-year-old Samuel Elltoft, was interrogated by detectives and soon broke down. He recalled how, George Sumner, had been brushing up in the shop as he watched Miss Bradfield counting the day's takings. Suddenly he had lost his temper and brutally attacked and raped the manageress, before beating her to death with a wooden baton. The distraught boy was overcome with emotion as he told how Sumner had bullied him into helping him dispose of the body, warning him that they would both hang if it was ever found. He explained how they had bundled the body into a sack and taken it by cart to the Leeds-Liverpool Canal, where they had dumped it.

George Sumner was finally captured by the police, after hiding out at a lodging house in St James Street. Tried at St George's Hall in February 1914, the brute was sentenced to hang. His young workmate, Samuel Elltoft, was found guilty of being an accessory to the horrific incident and was sentenced to four years' hard labour.

When May Shambrook read the details of the murder in the *Liverpool Echo*, a freezing cold shiver run through her as she realised that she had witnessed most of the grisly details of the case in her strange vivid dreams. This single instance of prophetic vision was inexplicable and, to her relief, she never encountered such a gruesome nightmare again.

FIRE ALARM

Another example of a nightmare becoming reality is to be found in the following sad story. In the early hours of one morning in 1979, a woman in Netherley named Maureen McAllister was suffering a bout of insomnia. She was so restless that her husband Jack was woken up by her fidgeting and asked her what was the matter. Maureen complained that she couldn't sleep and dragging herself out of bed, went down to the kitchen for a cigarette. As she was putting the kettle on, she heard a sudden noise outside. Entering the dark hall, she pulled aside the curtain covering the small window in the front door. What she saw was to haunt her for the rest of her life.

In the moonlight, she saw a hearse pull up at their door. How could this make sense? as the time was a quarter to four in the morning and even more importantly, no one had died. Next to the coffin she could see an elaborate floral tribute that spelt out the word 'mum'. She was unable see the driver of the hearse, who was just a motionless silhouette. Doubting the evidence of her own eyes, she ran upstairs to her husband jabbering like a mad woman. When she finally managed to wake him, she yanked him out of the bed and virtually pushed him down the stairs.

Jack McAllister sleepily squinted through the window of the front door and he too saw the sinister out-of-hours hearse parked ominously in the street. He hurriedly unbolted the door and slid off the security chain, but when the front door was pulled open, the McAllisters both saw that the hearse was no longer there. Jack walked to the front gate and looked both ways up the road, but could see only the parked cars belonging to the people in the street. There was no hearse to be seen.

That morning at five o'clock, Maureen McAllister finally drifted off to sleep but after just a few minutes she suddenly woke up again in a cold sweat. She had experienced a harrowing nightmare, in which a large building was on fire. She could see a bunch of outstretched arms reaching through the bars of a window, desperately trying to attract attention to their plight. Clouds of thick black smoke were billowing out through the window and the people inside were screaming and coughing. Maureen was restless for the remainder of the night, uncomfortably troubled by the strange occurrences disturbing her sleep.

"What a night!" she sleepily reflected over breakfast. "I feel even more tired than when I went to bed."

Later on, when her husband had gone to work, she was still wondering about the significance of the funeral hearse with the chilling floral tribute. Flashbacks of the distressing nightmare about the people in the fire kept on coming into her mind with horrible reality. Her reflections were interrupted later when the telephone rang. It was Maureen's friend in Manchester asking if she wanted to stay over with her the next week. Maureen decided she would love to go and so made the necessary travel arrangements that day. In her excitement, she put the frightening events of the previous night to the back of her mind. However, on the day on which she was supposed to visit her friend, Jack broke his arm on a building site. Maureen therefore chose to stay at home and look after him, despite his repeated attempts to persuade her to have a well deserved break with her friend in Manchester.

Shockingly, the very next day, Maureen's friend died in a ferocious blaze at Woolworths in Manchester, along with eleven other victims. It seemed that most of the victims of were overcome with the toxic fumes given off by the fire in the upholstery section. Maureen was overcome with grief for her friend. Whenever she had been to stay with her in the past, they had always paid a visit to Woolworths. Her recollections of that awful sleepless night, only weeks earlier, came to her mind and made her shudder. Maureen knew that, had she gone to stay with her friend, she too would have perished in that dreadful blaze.

THE HARLOW STREET GYPSY

The Romany people possess legendary powers of precognition and I once received an interesting telephone call at Radio Merseyside about the so-called, Harlow Street Gypsy. An elderly lady, Mrs Eleanor Cook, told me that her mother, who lived in Harlow Street in the Dingle in the 1930s, had employed a maid named Virginia, who was of Romany descent. Virginia predicted that Eleanor would marry twice during her lifetime – firstly to a red-haired man who would never reach the age of forty, and secondly to a man with a drooping moustache.

Eleanor subsequently married red-haired Charles Wright, who died suddenly, just a few days after his thirty-ninth birthday. The Romany's second prophecy also came true, when she married George Cook, who wore a distinctive droopy moustache, after two years of widowhood.

Virginia, who was still employed by Eleanor at the time of her second marriage, warned her new husband to avoid people bearing the names of Teddy or Peggy. George was something of a sceptic and considered this warning to be patently absurd. A year later, a Scottish couple moved into the house next door to the Cooks. When George learned that their Christian names were Edward and Peggy, he thought that it was nothing more than an amusing coincidence and happily accepted an invitation from them to attend their house-warming party.

An hour after sitting down at the table during the party, Mr Cook suddenly dropped his knife and fork and grabbed the edge of the table, obviously in severe pain. He asked to be excused, doubled up as he was with excruciating stomach cramps. He assured his wife that he would be fine once he had had a lie down, saying that it was probably nothing more than a bit of indigestion and he urged her to stay at the party, at least until she had finished her meal.

Later that evening, Mrs Cook, accompanied by Virginia, who had also been to the party, returned home and were alarmed to discover a trail of blood leading across the hallway and up the stairs. The trail led to the bedroom, where she found the inert body of Mr Cook, lying in a pool of blood. An autopsy revealed that he had bled to death from a burst stomach ulcer.

One day, some time after her husband's death, the subject of conversation in Mrs Cook's household turned to religion and the gypsy woman foretold that the Catholic population in the city would one day have an enormous round church built, with an unheard of sixteen spires on the top. Mrs Cook and the two other people present ridiculed the preposterous prediction, but Virginia may well have been referring to the Metropolitan Cathedral, which has does indeed have around sixteen spires, and is shaped like the crown of thorns. The Harlow Street Gypsy also predicted that the River Mersey would one day turn black – perhaps she had foreseen some future pollution incident, of which there have unfortunately been several.

WHATEVER HAPPENED TO MOTHER?

In 1889, a wealthy mother and her daughter from Heswall were returning from a holiday in India. They broke off the final leg of their journey in Paris, in order to visit the city's exhibition, booking a room at a large prestigious hotel. They signed their names in the register and were taken up to their room, number 342, a luxurious suite, with heavy plum-coloured drapes, exquisitely-designed velvet rose-coloured wallpaper and lavish furniture.

Almost as soon as they had tipped the porter and closed the door, the mother fell ill, becoming faint and dizzy. She was immediately put to bed and the hotel doctor urgently summoned to her room. After examining her, the doctor called for the manager and then proceeded to argue with him in French. Then the manager abruptly turned to the sick woman's daughter to relay a stark message.

"Your mother is seriously ill, Madamoiselle, and it seems that the only medicine that can help her is to be found at a doctor's surgery on the other side of Paris. We cannot leave her for a moment, so you must hurry at once to fetch the medicine yourself."

The girl was in no position to argue and set out at once by carriage for the address but had to wait for almost forty minutes at the surgery, whilst the medicine was made up. By the time she had returned to the hotel, almost two hours had passed. As she rushed into the hotel foyer, clutching the precious medicine in her hand, she spied the hotel manager and dashed up to him.

"How is mother?" she gasped earnestly.

The manager returned her entreaty with a blank stare. "Excuse me, Madamoiselle, but I have never set eyes on your mother."

"Of course you have," replied the exasperated girl. "We signed in this morning, right in front of you and then my mother fell ill. You must remember."

The manager raised an eyebrow but maintained his air of professional politeness and continued coolly, "You came here alone, Madamoiselle."

He then went over to reception desk and brought back the hotel register. He pointed to her signature and the girl could see that her mother's name was no longer there. The manager patiently watched as the confused English girl desperately flicked through the pages to search for her mother's signature but she could not find it. With rising panic, she took hold of the manager's arm and led him up to room 342 where she had left her sick mother. Upon opening the door of the room, the girl was startled to find that it bore no resemblance to the one she had seen earlier. Gone were the plum-coloured drapes and the rose-coloured wallpaper, gone, too, was the lavish furniture. Her first assumption was to suspect that the number on the door had been switched, but the manager allowed her to inspect every room on that floor and none of them looked anything like the original room 342. She ran downstairs and demanded to see the hotel doctor. Presently, the man who had treated her mother just two hours earlier came to see her, but he also denied ever meeting either her or her mother.

When the girl finally returned to England, alone, she told the authorities that she believed that her mother had been kidnapped in Paris, but they did not believe her incredible story and nor did anyone else. Two years later, she was committed to a lunatic asylum.

There are two main theories that have been proposed as possible solutions to the mysterious disappearance, which certainly took place because her mother's movements could be traced right up to just before she arrived at the hotel. Perhaps the woman had contracted a highly contagious disease whilst in India, which could have resulted in the Parisian authorities being forced to close down the hotel had the story come out. If this was the case, perhaps the hotel manager and the doctor had conspired to dispose of the woman – but how could they have redecorated and refurbished an entire suite of rooms in a mere two hours?

The other, even more remote possibility, is that the mother was some kind of undercover spy, involved in a covert espionage mission at the Paris Exhibition and was subsequently 'eliminated' by enemy agents. This is pure conjecture and would still not explain how the hotel room could have been so radically transformed in such a short period of time. The whole case seems to defy all rational explanation.

THE HUMAN HAND

From the earliest times, the symbol of the human hand has featured in the culture and occult folklore of many nations. To primitive people, the hand was regarded as something magical, because of its ability to create tools, weapons and cave paintings and there is an ancient record of primitive man's reverence towards the hand in the form of a cave painting depicting an open hand on the wall of a cave at El Castillo in Spain.

In the Book of Daniel in the Bible, we have the first written record of a live, disembodied hand:

In the same hour came forth fingers of a man's hand and wrote over against the candlestick upon the plaster of the wall of the king's palace. And the king (Belshazzar) saw the part of the hand that wrote.

On another occasion, it is recorded that Daniel was touched by a hand that set him upon his knees.

In the Arthurian legends, there is an account of how Bedevere threw Excalibur into the lake and watched in awe as a hand emerged from the waters and grasped the sword.

The cult of the hand really took off in the sixteenth century, when the practice of robbing the right hand of a hanged man became a popular routine for superstitious criminals. After an execution, these ghoulish miscreants would wait for darkness, then raid the gibbet in which a body had been left hanging. A ladder was placed against the gibbet and up would go the knife-wielding felon to hack off the hanged man's bound right fist.

The severed hand was later drained of blood and sealed at the wrist where a small wooden base was attached. Inserted between the second and third fingers of the dead man's hand was a candle made of human hair. Once lit, this unholy candle was supposed to ensure that all those who were asleep in a house being burgled would stay asleep. The logic behind this line of thinking seems ridiculous to the modern mind, but we must remember that, even today, there is a large proportion of the population which is gullible enough to believe in tabloid horoscopes – and this in the age of the computer!

Anyway, these hand charms were known as 'Hands of Glory' and the most famous incident of such a talisman being employed, occurred at Bowes Moor in North Yorkshire, around 1790.

One night, a woman arrived at the Old Spital Inn (which lies about halfway between Barnard Castle and Brough) and requested a room for the night. After supper, the woman settled down by the blazing fire for a while and started to doze. A maidservant then noticed that the female traveller was wearing what looked like men's trousers and they were showing from the bottom of her skirt. This naturally aroused her suspicions, so she also pretended to snooze in a chair by the fire, while she observed the mysterious traveller through partially-closed eyes. The man disguised as a woman, not realising that he was being observed, surreptitiously opened one eye and looked around, then produced a Hand of Glory from beneath his voluminous skirts. He lit the gruesome hand's hair candle and recited a spell that was said to unleash the talisman's power:

> *Let those who rest more deeply sleep.*
> *Let those awake, their vigils keep.*
> *Oh, Hand of Glory shed thy light,*
> *Guide us to our spoils tonight.*

The robber then opened the door of the inn in order to admit several accomplices, who had been lurking in the shadows outside. Before they could enter, however, the vigilant maid sprang up, ran to the door and slammed it shut. She bolted it and ran upstairs to wake the landlord and his family, but soon found that she could not wake them. As she shook them repeatedly, she could hear the gang of robbers outside, attempting to break down the door of the inn. Then she suddenly remembered that the only way to wake the sleepers from their unnatural sleep, was to extinguish the Hand of Glory candle, which was said to be impossible unless 'blue', or skimmed, milk was thrown over the flame. The maid raced to the kitchen, seized a bowl of milk and hurled it at the grizzly hand and successfully doused the candle flame.

At that precise moment, the sleepers awoke and the landlord quickly picked up his gun and went to investigate the source of the commotion. At that moment, the door of the inn succumbed to the battering and crashed inwards – but the landlord had reached the bottom of the stairs and blasted the intruders with his shotgun. They howled and fled into the night, peppered with shot!

❋ ❋ ❋

In the Lancashire town of Ashton-in-Makerfield, near Wigan, is another dismembered hand, mounted in a glass case in the church of St Oswald. However, this hand was not used for stealing, but for healing. The hand is the relic of St Edmund Arrowsmith, who was put to death in 1628 just for being a Catholic Priest.

Before St Edmund was hanged, his persecutors dragged him through the streets on a hurdle. Throughout his ordeal, the holy man clung on to two pieces of paper which contained the words of a prayer and an act of contrition. When his humiliating journey finally ended, he bravely mounted the ladder to the gibbet and was promptly hanged.

When Edmund was dead, the ghouls who were present cut him down, dismembered him, disembowelled and quartered him and tore out his heart. The priest's head was cut off and set on a pole amongst the pinnacles of a nearby castle. The judge who had sentenced him was very pleased with this butchery and, with a sickening grin, picked up the various dismembered parts of the priest and casually examined them. Then, suddenly, he remembered something that the priest had said to him during the trial. On sentencing the holy man, the judge had said, "You shall die!" over and over, and the priest had responded with, "And you, too, my Lord, may die."

At the time, the judge had dismissed the priest's words as a treasonable remark, but, just over a year after the execution, he was sitting at supper, when he felt a hard blow to his head, as if someone had struck him with a fist. The judge swung round and on seeing no one other than his old servant at the other end of the room, he felt quite frightened. He asked the servant if he had seen anyone strike him, but he was equally baffled, as no one had either entered, or left the room.

The next morning, the judge was found sweating in his bed with an expression of naked terror etched on his face and he died shortly afterwards.

Relatives of the martyred priest managed to recover his right hand from the grisly remains at the castle and brought it, as a token, to his heartbroken mother. At around the same time, it was discovered that people suffering from a variety of illnesses, who had touched the hand, became cured. The 'Holy Hand', as it came to be known, is still said to be affecting cures today. It is venerated in St Oswald's Church every Sunday afternoon at 3.30pm, when the priest blesses those who congregate with the relic.

NIGHT OF THE BLACK RATS

Beneath Mason Street, in Liverpool's Edge Hill district, there is a maze of tunnels. They are the work of Joseph Williamson, or the 'Mole of Edge Hill' as he is known in local folk lore. Although he was born into a poverty-stricken Warrington family in 1796, Williamson rose from the gutter by sheer determination and hard work to make a large fortune for himself in the tobacco trade.

After coming to Liverpool, the Mole devised Britain's first 'job creation scheme' in 1806, by employing large numbers of the destitute souls trying to survive the slump in the economy which had been caused by the exhaustive cost of the Napoleonic Wars. Williamson assigned the men numerous pointless tasks and the most famous senseless work which he commissioned was the creation of a vast labyrinth of tunnels carved into the sandstone strata of Edge Hill. None of the navvies who burrowed their way for miles through subterranean Liverpool had any idea what the tunnels were for – all they knew was that Williamson had paid them well to make them.

Today, a few of the tunnels are open to the public, but the majority lie empty and abandoned. Some are crumbling and others have been used for waste disposal and are full of rubble and refuse from various eras. This neglected subterranean network is a rat's paradise but in 1941, the detonation of a German landmine in Edge Hill caused a mass exodus of the rodent population. The landmine fell near Overbury Street, destroying St Anne's School. The blast burst the boilers in the school and a caretaker was scalded to death. The shock wave from the bomb simultaneously shook the sandstone bedrock of Edge Hill with a seismic jolt, causing thousands of rats to flee from their underground sojourn.

Later that night, an old man was walking down Mason Street, when he saw what looked like a black oil slick, advancing down the cobbled road. He assumed that the black mass was some spillage from a tank that had perhaps been ripped apart by the bomb-blast. Then he noticed the thousands of pairs of red specks twinkling in the seething black tide and, with mounting horror, realised that a plague of fat sewer rats was heading his way. Although he was seventy-three years old, he managed to shin a couple of feet up a lamp-post, just in the nick of time, as the sickening river of squeaking, red-eyed rodents swept past beneath him, inches from his boots.

When he looked to his right, he saw a vaguely amusing sight – a bunch of motley cats, perched precariously on a swaying tree branch, warily eyeing the swarming mass of rodents. The felines, being vastly outnumbered by the rats, wisely stayed put up the tree!

DEAD ON ARRIVAL

This weird incident allegedly happened at the new Royal Liverpool Hospital on Prescot Street in the early 1980s.

The double doors of the casualty department swung open one day and an unaccompanied man staggered inside with a badly bruised forehead and a bloodied nose. He managed to make it to the reception desk, where he informed the receptionist that he had just been involved in a car accident near Fraser Street and that he felt very peculiar. His actual words were, "I feel as if I am dead."

A nurse was called and she ushered him into a cubicle and

sat him down and told him to take off his jacket, but he refused, because he was too busy trying to take his own pulse. "I knew it! No pulse!" he declared, his eyes wide with fear.

The nurse eventually managed to calm him down sufficiently to be able to take his pulse herself. She firmly grasped his left wrist and lifted the watch on her apron in order to count the beats – but none could be detected! She was obviously deeply perturbed by this, since the man was living and breathing in front of her. Before she could either make another attempt, or call for assistance, her agitated patient stood up and marched back outside. As he passed through the swing doors, he said to a passing ambulance man, "I feel as if I am dead and the whole world died with me." Then he staggered off across the car park before anyone could stop him. It was not unusual for people to discharge themselves in this way and there was nothing the medical staff could do about it as we live in a free country.

Less than ten minutes later, the same ambulance man was called to the scene of a road traffic accident close to London Road. On arrival at the scene, he was confronted by the very same man whom he had seen earlier in A and E, but this time he was lying dead inside his vehicle. The postmortem established that he had suffered a massive heart-attack whilst at the wheel of his car and had crashed into a concrete lamp-post. His forehead was badly bruised and his nose was bloodied, but other than that there was not a mark on him. He was dressed exactly like the man who had visited casualty about ten or fifteen minutes before; a man who had obviously had a premonition of his own death.

DOUBLE JEOPARDY

In 1922, Peter Malone, a dockworker from Stanhope Street, became depressed after hearing that his estranged wife, living in Wales, had been murdered. Someone had strangled her in her bed. Despite their separation, Mr Malone was on good terms with his ex-wife, Liz, and often used to visit her with his best friend, William Jackson, a clerk. It was the latter who saw his friend acting crazily one day, on the fourth storey of a waterfront warehouse on the corner of Wapping and Sefton Street. Malone had opened a small window and was sitting on the ledge, gazing listlessly at the cobbled street over 150 feet below.

"Peter! What the hell are you doing?" Jackson asked, putting down the ledger he was working on.

"Contemplating suicide my friend," Peter Malone said in a low despondent voice.

Intermittent gusts of wind from the Mersey ruffled his curled hair as he carelessly dangled his legs over the ledge.

"Don't be a fool, Peter! Think about your children!" Jackson tried to talk sense into his friend, at the same time cautiously creeping towards the window.

"Stay where you are, Billy, or I'll take my life, I swear it." Peter Malone spat in agitation, as he leaned forward slightly and looked despondently at the ground far below.

"I won't let you take your life, Peter!" Jackson persisted, poised to make a grab at the suicidal man.

Then, just as Malone twisted round to look at his friend, his left thigh slipped sideways and he felt himself beginning to slide backwards off the ledge. His heart somersaulted and he heard his friend's voice scream, "No!"

"Oh! Jesus!" exclaimed Jackson. His friend was dangling

from the ledge by his fingers and his grip was slipping.

"Help, me!" Malone shouted desperately.

Suddenly, William Jackson's whole demeanour changed and his lips broke into a sly smile. He avoided eye contact with his friend as he edged closer. A short pause and then he silently took the last step over to the sill and began systematically prising Malone's fingers from the ledge.

"No! Billy! What're you doing?" screamed Malone.

"I killed your wife, Peter," Jackson announced with a tremor in his voice, still unable to look Malone in the eyes.

Malone could not comprehend the danger he was in. Unable to speak, he could only returned a stupefied expression. The harsh wind was now pounding against his face as he summoned every last ounce of strength to cling on to that ledge, because now that it was about to be taken away from him, life suddenly seemed so precious.

Jackson kept on talking, his tone becoming more and more controlled and embittered.

"I had an affair with her and she wanted me to leave Maureen, but I love my wife and kids." He stood up and trod heavily on the remaining desperate fingers. Jackson's voice quickened as he hastily explained, "I had to do it, or she would have told Maureen." His eyes were completely devoid of any compassion or emotion, as he kicked the last clutching fingers off the ledge.

Peter Malone plummeted to the ground like a stone. As he fell, he saw Jackson's cruel face watching him from over the ledge as he hurtled towards his gruesome fate. There was a dull, sickening thud as he hit the concrete, followed by an overwhelming deep sleep, so intense that even dreams were absent. Neurologists refer to this curious state as 'awareness'. The most chilling form of awareness is when a patient under anaesthetic remains conscious but paralysed, able to feel every excruciating scalpel incision but unable to communicate to anyone. Malone was lucky to feel nothing. His only sensation was that he was drifting out of his body for a while, a peculiar rising sensation, which went on for an incalculable time.

The next thing Malone knew, he was beginning to regain consciousness in a hospital bed. At first it felt like swimming through treacle, but gradually, day by day, he came back to life. By some miracle, he had survived the fall, but it had left him without speech and his sight was lost in his left eye. Imagine then, how Malone felt when he awoke one morning to see that one of his bedside visitors was the despicable murderer, William Jackson, who had had the audacity to bring him fruit.

At that stage, all Malone could do was make incoherent grunting sounds. He tried to point an accusing finger at the killer, but could scarcely lift his shattered arm. He was completely unable to reveal the identity and guilt of his evil visitor. Jackson seemed on edge as he whispered the same thing repeatedly in Malone's ear, "Peter, thank the Lord you survived. Do you remember me?"

Fearing for his life, Malone would only shake his head in response to this repeated question. Soon the day came when he suddenly regained the power of speech. It was during the dead of night. He cried out at the top of his voice and roused a nurse from her slumbers. She frantically ran into Malone's tiny room and then listened as he gave an emphatic and full account of the confession his so-called friend had made, and of how he had prised his fingers from the ledge, instead of offering a helping hand. The police were soon banging on the door of William Jackson's home in Toxteth's Fisher Street. His wife answered and explained to that her husband had been missing for two days. A search was immediately launched for the dangerous killer, but he was never found. There were rumours that he had fled to Ireland. Others said that he had gone to London and was hiding out in Whitechapel, but no one was certain.

Incredibly, Peter Malone made a full recovery from his appalling injuries. The blindness afflicting his left eye was found to be only temporary and after a long period of recuperation he slowly began to lead a normal life again. In the latter years of his life, when his children had left home and married, the old dockworker often expended his money in long drinking bouts in the taverns of the Dock Road. Despite his physical recovery, he never emotionally recovered from the terrible experience and when he died in 1946, he rambled on his deathbed about losing a wife and a friend, all in the name of love.

GLOOMY SUNDAY

In December 1932, a down and out Hungarian, Reszo Seress, was trying to make a living as a songwriter in Paris, but was failing miserably. All of his compositions so far had failed to impress the French music publishers, but he carried on chasing his dream nevertheless, determined to become an internationally famous songwriter. Seress and his girlfriend had constant rows over the insecurity of his precarious lifestyle. She urged him to get a full-time job, but Seress was uncompromising in his ambition. Telling her adamantly that he was going to be a songwriter or a hobo and that was that.

One afternoon, things finally came to a head. Seress and his fiancée had a fierce row over his utter failure as a composer and breadwinner and the couple parted with angry words. The next day, which happened to be a Sunday, found Seress sitting at the piano in his apartment as usual, gazing morosely through the window at the Parisian skyline. Outside, storm-clouds were gathering in the grey sky and soon the heavy rain began to pelt down.

"Typical gloomy Sunday," Seress muttered to himself, as he desultorily played about on the piano's keys. Then, quite suddenly, his hands began to play uncontrollably play and picked out a haunting and melancholy melody that seemed to perfectly echo the downhearted way he was feeling over his quarrel with his girlfriend, as well as reflecting the dispiriting weather.

"Yes! That's it! Gloomy Sunday will be the title of my new song," Seress exclaimed excitedly and grabbing a pencil, wrote the notes down on the back of an old postcard. Thirty minutes later he had completed the song, which was sent off to a music publisher and accepted straight away. The publisher told Seress that his song would soon be distributed to all the major cities of the world. The young Hungarian was ecstatic that he was finally achieving recognition he deserved.

However, a few months after Gloomy Sunday was printed, there were a spate of strange occurrences that were allegedly sparked off by the new song. In Berlin, a young man requested a band to play the tune and after the number was performed, the man went home and killed himself by shooting himself in the head with a revolver. He had apparently been complaining to relatives that he had become severely depressed because of a new song which he could not get out of his head. That song was later discovered to be Gloomy Sunday.

A week later, in the same city, a young female shop assistant was found hanging from a rope in her flat. Police investigating the suicide found a copy of the sheet-music to the jinxed song in the dead girl's bedroom.

Curiously, two days after that tragedy, a young secretary in New York gassed herself. Once again the mysterious song was implicated in the death, when, in a suicide note, she requested Gloomy Sunday to be played at her funeral. Only weeks after that, another New Yorker jumped to his death from the window of his seventh-storey apartment, after a neighbour had heard him playing the deadly song on his piano. Also, around the same time, a teenager in Rome who had heard the fateful tune jumped off a bridge to his death.

The newspapers of the world were quick to report other deaths associated with Seress's song. It seems that the dangerous song even affected listeners as far a field as Liverpool. In Toxteth one evening, a woman played a recording of Gloomy Sunday at full volume, infuriating and frightening her neighbours, who, like everybody else, had read of the widely-reported fatalities supposedly caused by the tune. As the night wore on, the stylus finally became trapped in a groove, causing the same piece of the song to play over and over again. This further incensed the neighbours, who hammered on the woman's door but there was no answer. Determined to stop the mournful and repetitive din, they forced the door open, only to find her stone cold dead, slumped in her chair having swallowed an overdose of barbiturates.

As the months went by, a steady stream of bizarre and disturbing deaths that were alleged to be connected to Gloomy Sunday song, finally persuaded the chiefs at the BBC to ban the seemingly accursed piece of music from the airwaves. The deadly tune was not heard again.

THE AFTERLIFE CLUB

This is a strange but true tale of subtle deception which took place in Liverpool and Bournemouth in the late 1870s. In 1879, army medical officer Robert Jones, died of natural causes. He was buried in St James Cemetery, leaving behind a thirty-nine-year-old wife named Violet. The marriage between Violet and Robert Jones had not exactly been a harmonious one. A tempestuous couple, they quarrelled frequently and Dr Robert Jones had been rumoured to have been having an affair with an eighteen-year-old maid named Nancy.

An odd thing happened one Sunday, just a week after Robert Jones had been laid to rest. Violet visited the cemetery carrying a wreath to place on her late husband's grave. She slowly gathered her thoughts as she approached the grave, still very upset by her sudden loss. Her attention soon became drawn to a sinister figure kneeling at the graveside in a long black coat. He was crouched up close to the stone, intensely poring over the inscription on the gravestone. The stranger wore a floppy fedora hat with the brim pulled down, concealing his eyes. Violet wondered if he was some distant relative of her late husband who had been unable to make the funeral, but when she approached, the man in black turned towards her and bolted right out of the cemetery, almost knocking her to one side without even acknowledging her. His abrupt departure made Violet feel uneasy and she drew her coat tightly around herself and tried to compose herself.

Months later, summer arrived and a shopkeeper named James Mooney started to pay attention to the widowed Mrs Jones. Within months they were courting, as Violet started to feel more like herself again after a depressing grieving period.

Seeking some privacy, the couple booked into a very small hotel in Rhyl, far away from the gossiping tongues of Violet's neighbours. It was a very hot night, so Violet asked James to open the window and the couple then cuddled comfortably back into bed. A gust of wind from the window suddenly happened to blow one of the curtains aside and they were startled to see a face revealed, peering in at them. Violet screamed hysterically because it was the face of robert Jones, her dead husband. James Mooney also saw the face and reluctantly went outside to try and apprehend the prowler, there was no sign of anyone there. Violet was positive that she had seen the ghost of her husband and became very agitated. She was unable to sleep that night, as she believed that he had returned from beyond the grave to haunt her and show his disapproval of her unseemly behaviour.

Just over a year later, Violet married James Mooney and they set off on their honeymoon to Bournemouth. Whilst walking along the pier at the sedate seaside resort, Violet and James noticed a man in a bowler hat, who seemed to be following them. James Mooney finally snapped and he confronted the man and a struggle ensued, during which the man's hat fell off. It was Dr Robert Jones. Back from the dead! In the flesh! A veteran of the Kaffir War, Jones knew how to take care of himself. He took a swipe at James Mooney and successfully floored him with a swift upper cut. As Violet witnessed the incomprehensible episode, she fainted, landing heavily on the jetty. As her new husband bent down to assist her, Jones sped away and vanished into the milling crowds. Mooney staggered to his feet and rubbed his chin. The force with which he had been hit had been very powerful, surely no ghost could throw a punch like that and he wondered what on earth was going on. Violet was equally bewildered and dismissed her sightings of her late husband as the result of an accumulation of stress and guilt caused by her recent wedding. Unsettled by it all, the couple avoided any discussion of the unfortunate events.

It was five years later that the most peculiar incident occurred, when Violet received a letter from her supposedly dead husband. It was a truly amazing letter, bearing a London postmark. In the letter, Dr Robert wrote that he was dying of cancer and went on to make a startling confession. He explained that he belonged to a group called the Afterlife Club and described how this was a group of people who had faked their own deaths and then paid coroners and doctors to falsify burial certificates and produce bogus coroners' reports. He went on to explain how, in some instances, the bodies of vagrants were placed in the coffin of the person who wished to fake his own death, in others, stones and slates had even been placed in coffins. It seemed that the man in black, seen by Violet at her late husband's graveside, had been none other than Dr Robert Jones himself, taking a vain look at the inscription on his own headstone.

In an attempt to justify his extreme actions, he confessed to Violet that he had faked his death in order to live with Nancy, the young maid, who had later deserted him. He had felt lonely and isolated and had therefore gravitated back to his wife. He had become intensely jealous when he saw Violet with her new love and, unable to suppress his jealousy, he had started to stalk her.

There were many other supposedly dead people who returned to life in this way. Some had faked death to escape debt, whilst others wished to start again with a new wife, and so escape the humdrum domestic routines of an unhappy marriage. Many members had left most of their savings to anonymous charities, which were actually just a front for the Afterlife Club. The club had been founded in the Lyceum, but even today, little more is known about the specific goings on that surrounded it.

ROCKING CHAIR GHOST

Rather appropriately, the following ghostly incident took place on the evening of 31 October 1974 – Halloween – the traditional time for ghosts to walk and witches to hold sabbats.

On that day, responding to the repeated requests of the people in the neighbourhood, two council workmen turned up at a derelict house on Edge Lane and began boarding up the broken windows. Gangs of children had been making mischief in the house and a series of fires had reduced it to a blackened shell. As one of the workman glanced through a hole in one of the grimy windows, he noticed a bespectacled old woman in a red cardigan, sitting in a rocking chair, knitting. He shouted to his mate, and then used his claw hammer to remove the board which he had nailed across the front door of the building.

When he stepped inside the house, there was no sign of the old woman, or of the rocking chair on which she had been sitting. After a quick search, the workman convinced himself that what he had seen had merely been a trick of the light and he and his friend quickly boarded up the door again. Nevertheless, just to reassure himself, he took one last peek through the broken window pane and was shocked to see the old woman sitting in the rocking chair once again, knitting away contentedly, as if she was in the comfort of her own home. He quickly called his mate to come and take a look but, as he did so, the ghostly old woman evaporated into thin air, along with her rocking chair.

Later that day, the workmen were packing up their tools and preparing to leave, when a woman from the neighbourhood approached one of them. "About time you boarded that eyesore up," she said. "It's a health hazard."

"Too right, love," answered the workman. "Oh! By the way. Have you got any idea who used to live there?"

"Some old woman. Never really knew her though; she was a bit of a recluse. Some days she didn't even open her curtains. The local kids used to torment her something rotten. One day they threw a stone at her window and broke it, then ran and hid and expected her to come out and chase them, like she usually did."

"And did she?"

"No. After a while they sneaked back up to the window and sneaked a look inside. There she was, slumped in her rocking chair, with her knitting needles and wool on her lap, not moving."

"Was she dead?" asked the workman, fascinated.

"Not half. Had been for some time. It was horrible. One of the kids screamed blue murder when he noticed a rat nibbling at the old woman's foot. Then the police broke in and apparently the place reeked. The coroner said she'd died from natural causes … been dead about four days. They said the rats had come up from the coal cellar and nibbled at her toes."

"Can you remember what this woman looked like when she was alive?"

"As I say, I didn't really know her, just remember she always wore the same red hand-knitted red cardigan.

This reply shook the workman to the core, as he realised that he had seen what must have been the ghost of the old woman through the crack in the window. Within minutes, he and his mate were back in their van, speeding away from the boarded-up house on Edge Lane.

PLOUGHBOY PROPHET

The word prophet usually conjures up visions of bearded biblical characters from the Old Testament, but in more recent times there have been secular-minded individuals who have had the talent, or some might say handicap, of seeing into the future.

One such seer was Robert Nixon, the Cheshire Prophet, an uneducated fifteenth century ploughboy. Robert was born in 1467, the only son of a virtually destitute Cheshire farmer. Farmer Nixon had long since resigned himself to the fact that his mentally disabled son would never amount to anything in life, so he had put him to use in the field as a ploughboy. The unfortunate lad was frequently made fun of by the locals and labelled 'the village idiot' because of the apparent slowness of his mind. His appearance also made him an object of ridicule as his head was unusually large and he had huge, protuberant eyes. Despite all the spiteful jibes he was subjected to, the ploughboy was good-natured and inoffensive and said very little to anyone beyond a simple "yes" or "no".

One day, out of the blue, Robert suddenly surprised everyone, by predicting that an ox belonging to a neighbouring farmer would die. Not long after he had uttered the prediction, he and a group of curious villagers watched as the healthy-looking ox in the next field collapsed. When the beast was examined, minutes later, no cause of death could be found.

News of the uncanny prophesy reached the ears of Lord Cholmondeley, who sent for Robert and kept him at his estate for a short while. The country squire tried to encourage the boy to learn to read and write, but Robert resisted all attempts at education, so eventually left the estate and ended up back at the handles of his father's plough.

A couple of days after leaving Lord Cholmondeley's estate, Robert was ploughing one of his father's fields, when he suddenly stopped mid-furrow and stared skywards with a gaping mouth. The farm overseer ordered him to get on with his work, but the ploughboy remained rooted to the spot, engrossed in something which he could obviously see in the clear blue sky. The overseer struck Robert with a strap and told him to stop daydreaming, but the boy was oblivious, and did not react.

For the space of an hour, the ploughboy stood gazing up at something in the heavens, which no one else could detect, until he finally broke out of his trance-like state and resumed his ploughing as if nothing had happened. The overseer was burning with curiosity and urged the lad to reveal what he had been staring at. Robert thought about it for a while and then replied enigmatically, "I have seen things that I cannot tell you and which man never saw before."

This enigmatic reply shook the overseer, who was used to the boy's monosyllabic utterances. Not only that, the ploughboy's voice had assumed a new clarity and speed of delivery, so unlike his usual muffled speech. It was almost as if something, or someone, was using the boy as a mouthpiece.

Further strange vocal deliveries from the farmer's son followed. One day, before a group of startled drinkers in the local tavern, Robert held forth for two hours, in the accentless voice of his mysterious alter ego, expounding theories about the "history of the future". This unbelievably comprehensive lecture included details about the rise of an individual named Oliver Cromwell, the Civil War, the subsequent beheading of Charles I, the Restoration of the Monarchy, the reign of William of Orange and the French Revolution. Towards the end of his epic discourse, Robert predicted the abdication of James II in 1688, "When a raven shall build its nest in a stone lion's mouth on top of a church in Cheshire, a king of England shall be driven out of his kingdom to return nevermore. As token of the truth of this, a wall of Mr Cholmondeley's shall fall!"

Lord Cholmondeley heard of the prediction and laughed it to scorn. He examined the wall mentioned in the ploughboy's prediction and, finding it to be completely sound, told his bailiff that young Robert would be wrong on this occasion. The bailiff laughed and nodded in agreement. However, the next day the apparently structurally-sound wall inexplicably crumbled to the ground. The remainder of Robert's prediction came true centuries later, when a raven did indeed build its nest in the mouth of a stone lion gargoyle at the top of a Cheshire church in 1688 – the day before King James II was deposed. The dethroned monarch later died in exile at Saint Germain in France.

On 22 August 1485, the Cheshire Prophet (as Robert Nixon was now known) was ploughing a field, when once again he angered his overseer by stopping abruptly in his tracks. Before he could administer his usual swipe with the strap, Robert suddenly lifted his whip and started brandishing it about, as if it were a sword.

"There, Richard! There!" he shouted. "Now! Up, Henry! Up with all arms! Over the ditch, Henry! Over the ditch and the battle is won!"

A gaggle of farmworkers came running across the field and gathered around Robert, who was now standing inert, with a smile on his face. He suddenly raised his whip in the air and declared, "The battle is over! Henry has won!"

The farmworkers fell about laughing at the ploughboy's amateur dramatics. But these same peasants had to think again when, two days later, two travel-weary messengers rode into the county of Cheshire bringing important news – King Richard III had died at Bosworth while fighting the Earl of Richmond, now King Henry VII of England. When one of the villagers asked the messengers the exact date on which King Richard had died, he was told that he met his death on 22 August, the date the Cheshire Prophet gave his performance of the remote battle, by simultaneously enacting the events at Bosworth.

On the day that the messengers arrived with the news of King Henry's victory, the ploughboy became extremely anxious and nervously asked several of the villagers if he could take refuge in their homes.

"Why? Who are you hiding from, Robert?" asked one bemused villager.

"The king's men!" he replied, "They're coming for me. They want to take me to the royal palace and if I go there, I'll die of thirst and starvation!"

The villagers could make no sense of the ploughboy's words, for they could not conceive of any possible reason for the king to want anything to do with the village idiot. And, for that matter, how would a guest starve in a royal palace?"

Yet, a few days later, several of the king's men rode into the Nixon farmstead looking for the famous Cheshire Prophet. When they caught up with Robert, they escorted him to King Henry, who was fascinated by the tales he had heard of the idiot-genius who could foresee the future.

The king assigned a scribe to accompany the ploughboy at all times and to record all of his predictions. One of the first prophecies to be recorded by the scribe concerned a future event in which soldiers, with white dust on their helmets, would invade the country through a tunnel.

Before setting out on a fortnight-long hunting trip, the king left instructions with his cooks to give the Cheshire Prophet all the food he desired. The cooks initially obeyed the king's commands but, after a few days, they tired of the ploughboy's incessant greed and decided to lock him up in a heavy oaken chest, until he was really hungry, just to teach him a lesson. In the hustle and bustle of palace life, the cooks completely forgot about the tiresome ploughboy. Two weeks later the king returned and asked if the Cheshire Prophet had made any more predictions whilst he had been away. Only then did the cooks remember that they had locked him up. With great trepidation, they rushed to the thick-timbered chest and opened it to find that Robert Nixon had died from thirst and starvation. The Cheshire Prophet's prediction of his own tragic death had come to pass.

A Ghost Calls

Those with a true clear conscience never fear a knock on the door after midnight.
Irish Proverb

There stands a large house in Abercromby Square which was once visited by a supernatural character. In 1845, the owners of the house, a Mr and Mrs Bickerstaffe, made preparations to go on holiday to Scotland. Mr Bickerstaffe left strict instructions with his staff not to admit any strangers while he and his wife were away. Mary Hennessey, the youngest housemaid, nodded in unison with the rest of the staff, as Mr Bickerstaff rambled on, giving out his various directives.

As soon as he and his wife were leaving the square in a hansom cab, Mary Hennessey poured herself a large glass of brandy and sat herself down in the kitchen with her aching feet resting on the warm hob, taking a well-deserved rest. The remainder of the staff decided to visit an inn, which stood in Mulberry Street, just around the corner, but Mary stayed behind to look after the house with the seventy-year-old butler, Mr Rumboldt.

At 9pm, the front door bell jangled and Rumboldt went into the Bickerstaffes' bedroom and peeped out of the window. He looked down at the caller with an expression of terror on his usually sangfroid face.

"Oh no!" he muttered to himself. "It's happening again!" and he rushed to the stairway and shouted to Mary. "Don't open the door whatever you do!"

But his warning came too late and Mary was already pulling the front door open. A tall woman, dressed in black, entered the house without invitation and pushed past the startled maid. Without a sound, the agile visitor seemed to glide up the stairs. As she neared the top of the first flight, she shouted, "The baby!"

Realising her mistake in opening the door, Mary trotted eagerly after the woman in black. The uninvited guest barged straight into an empty bedroom and let out a blood-curdling scream, terrifying young Mary. The sound of one of the sash windows being hastily opened echoed through the empty room – then a sickening thud was heard on the pavement outside.

"Mr Rumboldt! What has she done?" Mary shouted up to the drawing room.

Rumboldt emerged, visibly shaking.

"Nothing," he said. "Calm down."

Mary hurried down the stairs, yanked open the front door and ran down the steps outside, expecting to find the woman's mangled body on the pavement but there was nothing there. Mary craned her head and looked up at the drawing room window – it was still closed. The housemaid did not know what to make of it, until old Mr Rumboldt came down to explain.

"That was the ghost of Mr Bickerstaffe's first wife, Eve," Rumboldt said in a morose tone. "She came in one day because she heard the sound of Henry – her baby – choking to death in the room upstairs. It used to be the nursery. By the time she had climbed the stairs, Henry had turned blue and was already dead. The sight of her dead baby unhinged her and she threw herself out of the window and broke her neck in the fall. What you have just seen has happened several times before – the last time a few months before you were employed here."

Mary immediately decided that she was leaving, declaring that she had no intention of staying in a haunted house. However, Mr Rumboldt managed to persuade her to stay, by reassuring her that the apparition only seemed to turn up on the odd occasions when the house was mostly deserted. Indeed, Mary next saw the same heartbreaking reenactment two years later, when she was the only person in the house. On that occasion, the Bickerstaffes, the servants and the cook were all attending the funeral of Mr Rumboldt.

It is said that Mary Hennessey was later dismissed from her job because of an indiscretion; she unwisely told

Mr Bickerstaffe's second wife, and later widow, Florence, about the ghost and it turned out that she had not been aware that her husband had been to the altar before.

Today, the house that was once the Bickerstaffes' home is the property of Liverpool University, and several members of staff and security guards in this building have occasionally heard the front door bell ringing when there is no one on the doorstep – no one that can be seen that is!

KILLER IN THE BACKSEAT

In 1962 Susan Manley, a young woman from Hoylake, met and married her husband, an American. Subsequently she moved from her home town to start married life with him in Salt Lake City.

One bleak night in 1965, Susan was driving home from her mother-in-law's house in a place called Ogden, when, about three minutes into the journey, she glanced in her rear view mirror and happened to notice that a white car was following her. A rational woman, she remained calm, but kept her eye on the vehicle. Turning off abruptly to try and shake him off, she noticed that the other car had also turned. It then started to tailgate and whenever Susan speeded up, the mysterious car did the same.

Susan now began to panic. With horror stories of late night attacks haunting her mind, she leant over and locked the passenger door. In a desperate attempt to lose the predator, she took a winding route home, but to no avail as the car followed her down every lane and eventually on to the motorway. Suspicious and now afraid, Susan could not rid herself of the terrible feeling in the pit of her stomach. When she reached Salt Lake City, she even started speeding through red lights to get away from the white car, but it relentlessly copied her every move.

Home at last, but as Susan pulled hastily into her driveway the menacing car pulled up along side her. By this stage she was in a state of near hysteria, so she slammed her fist down on the car-horn. After some moments, her husband ran out of the house and became alarmed when he saw the state she was in. He angrily confronted the other driver, "What the hell is going on here?" he demanded, as the driver scrambled to open his door.

The driver's face was pale as he rushed from his car and tried to grab hold of Susan, who was still sitting, quivering in her front seat, with the doors firmly locked. She tearfully pleaded with her husband to do something, hastily explaining that the man had followed her all the way from Ogden. Her husband grabbed the stranger by the lapels of his jacket. As he did so, the man tried to explain himself, "I followed your wife because I was going to work ..." he gasped as Susan's husband shook him roughly. "... As I got into my car, I saw a man sneak into your wife's car, just before she reached the car park. Why don't you check if you don't believe me."

Dubiously, Susan's husband loosened his grip on the stranger to yank open the back door of his wife's car. To the total surprise of both Susan and her husband, there crouched a young man with a shaven head. He was squatting behind the front seat, clutching a knife as he giggled insanely to himself.

It turned out that the young man in the back seat was dangerously mentally unbalanced and had been on the run from a local psychiatric hospital for over a week. During that time he had slashed a vagrant's face and had also stabbed a dog to death in a frenzied attack. Susan, although shaken at the time, was grateful to the man who had followed her and indeed saved her from such a perilous situation.

This true story is no doubt the originator of many urban legends concerning the 'killer in the backseat'.

AN ACCUSING FINGER

One fine spring morning in 1849, twenty-nine-year-old music teacher Ann Hinrichson placed a notice in the front parlour window of her home at Number 20 Leveson Street, Toxteth: 'Furnished Apartments to Let'. Her Danish mariner husband, John, was away at sea, therefore she was left for a good while with the task of running a household and rearing their two sons, five-year-old Henry George and three-year-old John Alfred. She was also heavily pregnant with their third child. The only other person living at the house was the pretty young maidservant, Mary Parr.

Within days, twenty-six-year-old Irishman John Gleeson Wilson answered the advertisement and called at the house to inspect the vacant rooms – the front parlour and back bedroom. Finding them to his liking, he paid a week's rent in advance and moved in immediately. The following morning, at 11 o'clock, Mrs Hinrichson went to the greengrocers in St James Street and ordered some potatoes. She then visited the chandlers to purchase two jugs, before heading home.

Later that afternoon the errand boy arrived at her house laden with the potatoes. Unusually, Wilson answered and received the delivery; his manner was abrupt as he hastily grabbed the delivery. Thirty minutes afterwards, the delivery boy from the chandlers turned up with the jugs and rang the bell. This time there was no answer. The boy peeped through the keyhole and saw what seemed to be two legs lying across the hall. His curiosity triggered, he scaled the railings to look through the front parlour window. The scene that faced the boy resembled an abattoir. In large scarlet pools lay the bodies of Mary Parr and little Henry. The errand boy jumped down and, dizzy with shock, ran to find a policeman. He found one in Great George Street and the two hurried back to the house of carnage.

At around this time a little girl had arrived at the house for a music lesson. She also sensed something was wrong when she received no answer and a concerned neighbour smashed a window to gain access to the house. Within minutes, the policeman as well as crowds of people from the street, were swarming into the Hinrichsons' home. Mrs Hinrichson was found lying battered and stabbed in the hallway. In the parlour they found the maidservant, Mary Parr, suffering from horrific head injuries. She was still alive, but only just. Henry, the five-year-old tot lying beside her, was dead and coated in blood, a sight that forced a gasp from all who witnessed it. Down in the cellar, Ann Hinrichson's other son, John, also lay beaten and dead. His throat had been savagely cut from ear to ear.

The only clues to the abominable crime were a bowl of bloodstained water in John Gleeson Wilson's room, with a poker and tongs lying nearby, as well as the absence of a large sum of money belonging to Mr Hinrichson. The murderous lodger was nowhere to be seen.

Mary Parr was rushed to the Southern Hospital, where she slowly regained consciousness. She weakly managed to murmur that it was Wilson who had wiped out the family in cold blood, before slipping into a coma from which she never recovered. Within the hour, much police attention was focused on the horrific crime that was to shock the whole of Merseyside.

Wilson had sold several items from the robbery in a London Road pawnshop. Buying a disguise, he then fled to his former home in Tranmere, gloating as he escaped past the local police, who failed to recognise him as he boarded the Mersey ferry.

Wilson was smugly certain that he had escaped. However, on his first night back home, something very strange occurred. He sat greedily counting the money with the help of his estranged wife, who silently and fearfully suspected that he was the fiend behind the massacre in Toxteth. All of a sudden, his face turned ashen and he gasped out loud. Wilson had seen the face of an old man looking through the window, which should have been impossible, as they were on the second floor. The ghostly man was pointing at him with an accusing finger. Wilson's ex-wife also saw the apparition and screamed out in terror. The phantom vanished for a while but was seen three more times that night. The third time, it materialised at midnight over the couple's bed, wearing a judge's goat-hair wig.

Wilson fled from the house and at first light returned to Liverpool. He entered the pawnshop of a Mr H Samuel, in Great Howard Street, to sell a watch, but Mr Samuel's intuition told him the customer was the country's most wanted murderer and contacted the police. Wilson was taken into police custody, where he broke down under intense questioning and made a full confession. He was hanged in September of that year in front of 50,000 spectators. Interestingly, it is believed that his Tranmere house, where the ghost was seen, was once the home of an old judge …

FIVE O'CLOCK SHADOW

Most people who enjoy ghost stories and folk tales are well-accustomed to so-called urban legends. These are dubious stories that appear in a variety of versions. Examples of such tales are the totally unfounded claims that mice have been found in bottles of popular soft drinks, that Paul McCartney died in 1966 and was replaced by a look-alike who is still acting the part and so on. Such modern legends may seem harmless enough, but some tales can be libellous towards people and companies. For instance, in the late 1970s McDonald's had to officially denounce the widespread (and unfounded) rumour that the meat in its Big Mac hamburgers was being supplemented by worms! It was, of course, pointless for McDonald's to explain that, pound for pound, worms were actually more expensive than beef.

One popular urban legend that is usually passed off as a real incident which happened to a 'friend of a friend', may have had its origins in the following true story, which happened in Liverpool in 1949. Being a major port, stories told by word of mouth in Liverpool soon travel the world and this is a case in point.

Appropriately enough, the date was 31 October 1949, the night of Halloween, when forty-year-old motorist William Charnock, of Ennismore Road in Old Swan, decided he would visit his Aunt Verity in Knowsley. Charnock had to wear glasses when he drove, but couldn't find his specs anywhere, so he foolishly set out without them. While he was travelling along Prescot Road on his way through Knotty Ash, he saw a woman in a long black dress standing at the side of the road, waving at him. He slowed the car and pulled up to see what she wanted. Winding down the window on the passenger door, the woman peeped in and in a foreign accent said, "Please could you take me to Manchester?" Charnock explained that he was only going as far as Knowsley, but the woman did not seem to understand. She leant her head to one side and looked at him quizzically. So he opened the door and she climbed in.

"Oh! Thanking you, kind man," she said, in a slightly gruff voice, slamming the car door rather hard.

During the journey, Charnock learned that the woman had come to Liverpool from Sweden by boat and had been trying to trace relatives in Knotty Ash. She had been unable to find them and had been told by their former neighbours that they were now living in Manchester.

Charnock could not help making furtive glances at the woman, sensing that there was something strange about her. Her hands were rather large and the fingertips broad and square. Also, her straight brown shoulder-length hair seemed to have a synthetic texture. Despite not having his glasses on, he also noticed that the woman had a five o'clock shadow of stubble, which was showing through the heavy make-up. In fact, the stranger was obviously a man in drag and Charnock began to feel very uneasy. He wondered what was in the mysterious handbag – a knife? a gun? – or was he just being paranoid? Was the passenger merely an inoffensive transvestite? He tried to be rational but could not lose the distinct sense of fear he felt.

Charnock quickly concocted a plan to get rid of his dubious passenger. Thoughts flashed through his mind: if he could maybe pretend that his rear lights were on the blink, he could ask the stranger to go out and see if they were working, giving him the chance to drive off. Furthermore, if he left the handbag in the car as he went to check the lights, Charnock would even be able to drive off with it and see if there was a weapon in it or not.

Now convinced this plan was his only escape, he slowed the car to a halt in a secluded lane in Knowsley, just ten minutes from his aunt's house. He feigned concern as he studied the dials on the fascia.

"What is the matter?" the odd passenger inquired.

"The rear lights circuit. I think they're off. Could you get out and have a look to see if they are working?" Charnock asked, his pulse racing.

The female impersonator returned a blank look, "What for?"

"Just to see if the lights are working," Charnock explained, suddenly realising that sweat was trickling from his forehead.

"You go," the stranger bluntly suggested.

"Yes, of course," muttered Charnock. He reluctantly had to go along with his own ruse, so he left the vehicle to make a false inspection of the rear lights. He considered just making a run for it, but the nearest police station was over a mile away and there was no one about to come to his aid. On top of all that, dusk was falling fast. Charnock reluctantly returned to the car and after telling the eerie hitcher that the rear lights were working fine, he drove off.

Then events took an unexpected turn. A drunk stepped out into the path of the car, forcing Charnock to swerve to avoid him. As a result, the car collided with the stump of an old tree and was hurled into a 180-degree turn, until it juddered to a halt against the fence of a field. The androgynous man was thrown forward, causing him to hit his head on the dashboard. The impact dislodged his wig and the man shook his balding head, and looking sideways at Charnock with an expression of pure hatred, he reached for his handbag. Within a few moments bright car headlights approached the crashed car and Charnock exclaimed with relief, "The police!"

The man in drag squinted at the blazing headlamps coming steadily down the road, then suddenly fled from the car. His long legs, clad in stockings, easily cleared the fence and he vanished into the dark fields.

William Charnock sighed with relief as the car came towards him, but it couldn't have seen him because it failed to stop. It trundled on by, oblivious to the crash and continued on down the road, deserting him. He leaned forward to lock the passenger and tried the engine. Nothing! He tried again and this time it made a more hopeful sound but still would not start. He was desperate to get away, just in case the demented drag artist should return.

And he did return, seconds later. As Charnock tried desperately to start the car, the maniac in female attire screamed like a banshee and produced a knife, which he used to stab at the windscreen and offside door. The insane man tried to open the door, wrenching so hard on the handle that the vehicle rocked on its suspension. Perhaps it was that that loosened something in the engine, because it suddenly revved to life and Charnock tore off down the road. He could not be certain, but in his panic he thought he might have pulled the transvestite along the road for several yards.

When Charnock reached his aunt's home, he gave a rushed account of his ordeal and telephoned the police, who duly turned up and analysed the scrape marks on the car's bodywork. The wig that had fallen from the creepy assailant was found in the car and was the only concrete piece of evidence to back Charnock's incredible story. A detailed statement was taken from him, but the strange hitch-hiker was never found. Police began to wonder if the story had been a wild attempt at a Halloween hoax, but two other people later came forward to substantiate the account given by Charnock. Two dock workers claimed that a suspicious masculine-looking woman had passed them in one of the yards near the Trafalgar Dock. Their description matched Charnock's, right down to the handbag. Much effort was made to find the violent attacker, including enquiries at psychiatric hospitals in the north of England, but there were no reports of missing inmates.

The knife-wielding stranger had literally vanished from existence. However, he was allegedly encountered again on Prescot Road in 1951 and again in 1960, but police evidently failed to take either of the reports seriously, for on each occasion, the hitch-hiker had been reported on the last day of October, Halloween.

KATIE

In February 1876, forty-five-year-old Liverpool spinster Elizabeth Corte died at her home in Aigburth Road. A paraplegic from birth, and wheelchair-bound all of her life., Miss Corte had been cared for by her younger brother, Frederick, along with numerous servants. At her sad end she had finally succumbed to leukemia. Elizabeth and Frederick were originally from Tranmere, but had moved to Aigburth after their father's death in 1869. Their mother had also died, tragically, in a house fire many years before and the two orphans had been exceptionally close.

Frederick, a thirty-four-year-old bachelor, felt lost without his sister. The only other company he had was the elderly maidservant Jane Siddon and the similarly aged butler Archibald Smith, known affectionately as 'Smithers'.

Life was unbearable without Elizabeth and Frederick began to take refuge from his sorrows in a daily bottle of gin. During his excessive drinking bouts, he would wallow in self-pity and rant in a raised voice about life's injustices. Why did Elizabeth have to die? Why was he alone? Jane and Smithers would retreat to the basement kitchen whenever their master flew into such drunken rages. However, that spring something took place which was to change the grim outlook of the bereaved bachelor forever.

One gloomy morning, consumed with hatred and in a drunken haze, Frederick was throwing his deceased sister's wheelchair down the flights of stairs and barking at the maid to open the vestibule door. She obediently opened the front door, as Frederick got ready to hurl the wheelchair out into the busy street. As he lifted it, he noticed a barefoot girl with an angelic face blocking his way. She shivered on the doorstep, chilled by the March morning wind. Her scrawny arms cradling a bunch of drooping daffodils. "Out of the way!" Frederick snapped at her, raising the wheelchair six or seven inches off the ground ready to throw it.

The girl, who was aged about nine or ten, stepped aside and cast him a strange look; a look which began to thaw Frederick's heart. He felt more like the child. Refraining from throwing out the wheelchair, he instead smiled and stooped over the diminutive flower seller. "What do you want, little Miss?"

"I'm selling flowers, sir," the beautiful child told him, glancing at the wheelchair in confusion. "Please sir, if you don't it, I know an old man who'd be very grateful of it."

"Oh, is that so?" Frederick slurred.

The girl blinked a pair of large green eyes, shiny and watery with the biting wind, but she said nothing. Holding her timid stare, Frederick announced: "I'll buy all your flowers. Come in, come in." He backed into the hall, awkwardly manoeuvring the wheelchair. Behind him stood Mrs Siddon, wearing a look of unbridled disapproval. The little urchin remained rooted to the spot, full of suspicion, "Come on!" Frederick's voice boomed down the hallway, as the maid reluctantly beckoned the child in with a single tilt of the head.

The girl cautiously stepped with her hard-soled feet on to the luxurious carpet. Frederick treated the malnourished mite to a full English breakfast. She ate with her hands, despite the dissenting tutting of Mrs Siddons, but Frederick found it all very amusing. He learnt that the young girl's name was Katie Corrigan. She claimed she was an orphan at first, but later slipped up and mentioned her father. She admitted that he was a drunken bully who thrashed her and made her stand on the streets selling flowers picked from the park. Frederick decided that the unfortunate girl was to be clothed like a princess. He made a long list of items that were to be bought: shoes, dresses, petticoats and even ribbons to lend a measure of neatness and respectability to Katie's wild honey-coloured hair. Mrs Siddon measured her feet and the small circumference of her tiny waist. Smithers scribbled down the measurements and was afterwards given a small fortune to purchase the clothes and shoes.

Meanwhile, Katie was washed down in a bathing tub in the kitchen. When she was stripped, the maid recoiled in at the scars and weals that criss-crossed the poor child's back and Frederick was immediately informed. On hearing the sickening details, he quizzed Katie about her address, for he wished to inform the authorities of her barbaric father's whereabouts.

It seemed that Mr Corrigan resided in a dismal court off Mill Street in Toxteth. However, he was not there when Frederick Corte called to confront him. A helpful neighbour accompanied him to a nearby public house, where the brute spent most of his time. Frederick found him lying unconscious on the floor in the sawdust. Two inebriated women were giggling and trying to lift the child-beater.

Frederick knew it would be pointless trying to confront Corrigan in such an intoxicated state, so he returned home. On the way back, he thought about Corrigan's drunkenness and it made him fully realise how the horrors of drink had actually affected him. Later that day, the butler returned with the new clothes and Katie was transformed from a barefooted specimen of neglect, into a pretty and promising young lady. She was overwhelmed with excitement when she was brought before a full length mirror.

Kneeling beside her, Frederick tearfully clenched her hand. "Katie, if we asked you to stay with us, would you?" he asked in a broken voice.

Katie returned a puzzled look, as did the maid and the butler. Frederick looked at them, blinking to stem the tears welling up in his eyes. "She could stay here, couldn't she? She doesn't have to return to … to him."

"But, sir, we have no right to take her. We should inform the police about her father," argued Mrs Siddon, in a rational tone.

Smithers said nothing, but his sympathetic eyes spoke volumes as he surveyed Katie, who stood there, studying the novelty of her shiny buckled shoes.

"Katie, please stay," Frederick pleaded again. This time a tear escaped and rolled down his face. "You can have anything your heart desires."

The girl agreed with repeated nods and the two

embraced. This was the daughter he had longed for, for so many years. Tutors were hired to teach the girl and she showed a remarkable talent for the piano. Within a fortnight she was playing Für Elise. She also performed elaborate dances which melted the hearts of her substitute family. The child settled in well, radiating contentment. Whenever she became excited, she would perform one of her comical dances or play Für Elise, to the delight of her companions.

She was an inquisitive youngster, eager to know all the details of Frederick's life. Why wasn't he married? Was he in love with a woman? Had he ever been in love? The harsh circumstances the girl had been raised in had robbed her of a normal childhood and left her with a mature head on young shoulders. Frederick himself seemed to forget how young she was and would often find himself confiding in her. He disclosed that he had feelings for a widowed woman named Gloria. The girl asked him if he had expressed his feeling towards the widow.

"That just isn't done Katie" Frederick explained to her, sadly. "She lost her husband not more than six months ago."

His glance drifted out of the window.

Katie urged him to take flowers to Gloria, but Frederick's reply was as stubborn as before, "That just isn't done."

"A faint heart never won a fair lady," Katie had wisely told him, which made him laugh. Where had the young girl heard that quaint phrase, he wondered, but it made him ponder over the lonely course he was taking through life.

Meanwhile, Katie was soon reported missing by her father. The police surmised that the worst outcome had taken place. Weeks elapsed without a word and Frederick hastily made preparations to move to a residence in the north of the city.

However, Katie became homesick and one afternoon sneaked out of the house. Her father was astounded when he saw the girl so dressed up and angrily interrogated her about her three-week absence. Knowing that her benefactor would get into a lot of trouble if she gave any details about her unplanned sojourn, Katie claimed that she had been staying with a generous old lady in Birkenhead.

Taking full advantage of the circumstances, Corrigan took his daughter to the pub, pretending to cry with relief. For a while this play acting elicited offers of a drink, but the act soon wore thin. Katie's clothes were soon pawned and before long she had returned to her pitiful state, collecting firewood for her father to chop up and sell.

On Christmas Eve of that year, Frederick Corte saw Katie in Bold Street with her father and older sister. Corrigan was drunkenly singing and Katie was gazing into a shop window at the fine lace dresses that she had once worn, reflecting on the vastly different life she had once briefly led.

"Katie," Frederick gasped, when he saw his lost 'daughter'.

The girl turned and her mouth fell open with surprise as she recognised him. Oblivious to Corte's presence, Corrigan turned and grabbed Katie by the wrist. "Come here, you dawdler!" he slurred, as he dragged her away. Frederick tried to utter her name again, but was so choked up that the words died in his throat. His heart ached with sadness as he watched the girl who had been a shaft of sunlight in his grey world, walking away from him. Until the Corrigans vanished into the crowds of seasonal shoppers, he could see the pale face of Katie periodically turning back to look at him.

Back at the house, which now seemed so empty and lifeless, Frederick despondently tore down the Christmas decorations and had the tree thrown out. The house once again was overshadowed by his despairing mood. But the worst was still to come. Unable to forget Katie, a month later, in January 1877, Frederick Corte donned an anonymous Ulster overcoat and put on a flat cap. He walked to the dingy court near Mill Street, where two men were transporting a small wooden box to a cart. The box looked like a child's coffin. Moments later, Mr Corrigan emerged from the court with just one daughter. Not Katie.

"Who has died?" Corte asked a bystander, hoping against hope that the patent, terrible truth could be a misunderstanding. "His daughter, Katie," came the reply.

"The cholera," announced an old woman standing behind him.

Frederick Corte felt numb. He did not even notice the tears pouring from his eyes as he watched the little wooden box being heartlessly shoved on to the back of a horse drawn cart. For weeks, he once again drowned his sorrows in a bottle of gin.

Salvation came his way one spring day when he noticed the daffodils in Sefton Park. He thought of little Katie, about her hardships, and his mind drifted on to her advice regarding Gloria. For some reason that beautiful child had wanted him to be happily married. Her wise words echoed through his mind. Feeling indebted to the girl, the he felt that the least he could do was attempt to make his and Katie's wishes come true.

So Frederick Corte paid a visit to Gloria one evening and laid open the contents of his heart. He expected rejection, but Gloria was flattered and, after a brief period of courtship, she became engaged to marry Frederick. The couple soon married and honeymooned in Paris. On the night of their return from France, something inexplicable occurred. Frederick kissed his wife good night in their bed and was about to fall into a much-needed slumber, when he heard a distant sound. Gloria sat up as she also heard the noise drifting into their room. It was the faint strains of a familiar piano piece which Frederick recognised as Beethoven's Fur Elise, the piece of music Katie would play when she was happy.

BLOODY MARY

This is a grisly tale, told from two different sources; a man who worked at the Geemanco factory in Bartons Lane, Fazakerley in the 1960s – and a ouija board.

Before I begin, just let me issue a warning to the idly curious about misusing the ouija. Just as astronomy books warn amateur astronomers not to glance at the sun through their telescopes, I am warning novice dabblers to steer clear of meddling with the power of the ouija. I have seen so many lives wrecked by the upturned glass and even one suicide, that I must dissuade people from dabbling with forces they do not comprehend or respect. Now that I have got that off my chest, let's get on with the story ...

In early 1996 I was observing a ouija session in south Liverpool and the glass kept spelling out a girl's name. The surname of this girl was very unusual and stuck in my mind. I scribbled the name down together with what her spirit had to say, with my usual unbiased attitude. She described how she was caught between this world and the next because she had died after being struck on the head in a factory in Fazakerley in the late 1930s.

I decided to research the story and, a week later, I was tracing people who had worked at this factory through a friend who put me in touch with a man named John who had worked there in the 1960s. At that time it was called

Geemanco and was a printing works. John remembered that when he started at the factory, the guards seemed afraid to go near an old storeroom after dark, referring to an apparition they nicknamed Bloody Mary. He was curious about the nickname and asked why the ghost was so called. "Oh, you'll see, lad. You'll see," said an old guard.

About a fortnight later, John was working on the night shift and could not help noticing that his workmates and manager were becoming increasingly uneasy as the night closed in. John needed to go into the old, poorly-lit storeroom at around 1pm to fetch some paper – and there she was! A young woman, with a chalk-white face and blonde hair, in clothes that belonged to the 1930s. Her blonde hair was soaked in blood and there were scarlet streaks down her face and neck. Her eyes rolled upwards and her mouth quivered. John still recalls the paralysis which gripped his legs. "They just turned to jelly and I seemed to turn away from the ghost, which was about ten feet away, in slow motion. All I could say was, No!"

John finally regained control of his legs and described how he sped out of that storeroom at such a rate that he would have put Linford Christie to shame. The manager and his workmates calmed him down and reassured him that the storeroom was empty but he noticed that none of them would volunteer to go and switch the light off. For weeks after the encounter, John experienced terrible recurrent nightmares about the ghost, often waking in the night in a cold sweat, screaming out loud.

When I told him about the girl's name coming through the ouija, John poured himself a large Scotch with a trembling hand and gulped it down in one go. He had given up cigarettes for six months, but was suddenly rifling through his wife's handbag for her packet of

Embassy Regal. I went on to tell him that, back in the 1930s, a girl had been killed in that storeroom. She had been a factory worker, operating a large machine with an enormous eight-foot-long lever. This lever had developed a mechanical fault in its spring and one day it came crashing down without warning on the girl's head. One witness graphically described how the heavy lever had smashed open her skull, as if it were an eggshell. Amazingly, the girl did not drop dead on the spot but staggered around for a full ten minutes in a cataleptic state. Blood was gushing from the open wound in her head and her eyes were rolling about. The poor thing was unable to speak and presented a gruesome spectacle, terrifying her workmates.

A priest and a psychic were sent to the factory site some time afterwards and between them managed to induce her troubled spirit to move on from the place of her traumatic death, to what we would call the 'other side'. The terrifying ghost of Bloody Mary has not been seen since.

THROUGH A GLASS DARKLY

Mirrors are the windows of the devil
Leon Garfield

The following tale of prophecy has been circulating the south end of Liverpool for years. There are several different versions and, although each variation of the story gives different character names, the name of Mrs Prentice is always amongst them ...

On the night of 14 April 1912, the *Titanic* struck an iceberg in the North Atlantic, on her maiden voyage and sank, with the loss of 1,513 lives. When news of the unprecedented maritime tragedy reached Liverpool, everybody, especially the relatives of those who perished, was saddened and deeply shocked. The exception was Catherine Prentice, an elderly spinster, who lived in Upper Parliament Street, in the south end of the city. Mrs Prentice was regarded by her neighbours as something of an eccentric, as she always dressed in out-of-date clothes from the late Victorian period and the curtains of her home were always tightly drawn. It was rumoured that she dabbled in the occult and some even suspected her of being a witch. One of her few friends was Mary Orme, an independent widow, who ran a local chandler's shop.

A few months before the *Titanic* made her doomed voyage, Mrs Orme told Mrs Prentice that her eldest daughter Grace was emigrating to the United States and would be making her passage on the luxurious White Star liner. When Mrs Prentice heard the name of the liner, she turned ashen and in a broken voice warned Mrs Orme that Grace must cancel her voyage at once. Mrs Orme was naturally quite disturbed by her entreaty and asked if she thought something awful was going to happen to the liner.

Mrs Prentice foretold that the ship would sink after hitting an iceberg and that there would not be enough lifeboats to save all the passengers. Mrs Orme had long accepted that her friend had the gift of second sight and so took the chilling warning to heart. She pleaded with her daughter not to board the world's largest and most modern liner, but Grace was adamant that she would go and stubbornly refused to bend to her mother's request, saying that she was worrying unnecessarily. After all, it was a well-known fact that the *Titanic* had been described by her owners as unsinkable.

A fortnight before the doomed vessel was due to leave Southampton, Mrs Orme hid all Grace's savings from her as a last resort. This drastic measure had the required effect, but caused a bitter row to erupt between mother and daughter. However, when the appalling news of the great liner's sinking hit the headlines, Grace shuddered with relief.

In 1917, Mrs Prentice suffered a major stroke, which virtually robbed her of her powers of speech. Her condition later worsened to such an extent that she became bedridden. As she had no next of kin, she was cared for by her only friend, Mrs Orme and her daughter.

One night, Grace became tired of sitting at Mrs Prentice's bedside; she seemed to be unconscious and so she set off on a prying tour of the house. In an upstairs room she came across a crystal ball in the middle of a table which was covered in astrological charts of some kind. Fascinated, Grace tiptoed into the room and seated herself at the table and stared deep into the crystal ball. After a while, disappointed at seeing nothing, she grew bored and decided to have a browse through a bookcase of esoteric tomes of the occult, but these too were too obscure to be of interest.

She was about to leave the room, when she noticed a reversed, oval-shaped picture hanging on one of the walls. Her curiosity was aroused and she turned the picture frame around. She soon discovered that it was not a picture at all, but a mirror. She gazed at her reflection for a moment, then saw a dark shape glide across the glass, making her jump. Seconds later, the face of a man wearing a white tin hat appeared in the mirror. This apparition really frightened her and she stumbled backwards in alarm. The man's face appeared to be talking but, although his mouth was moving, no sound was audible. Then the face vanished and a succession of other images appeared in the mirror, including something which sent her fleeing from the house in panic.

When she arrived back home, crying and shaking, Mrs Orme immediately assumed that Mrs Prentice had died, until Grace told her about the ghostly faces in the weird mirror. Mrs Orme was furious at her daughter's prying and sharply told her that she should stop making such a fuss; she was simply overtired and imagining things.

Not long afterwards, Mrs Prentice passed away and, a couple of years after that, Mrs Orme and her daughter moved to Scotland Road, where they opened a small grocery shop. During the May Blitz of 1941, the two of them were sheltering in the cellar of the shop during an air-raid, when the building above them suffered a direct hit, raining bricks and debris down on their heads.

After the 'All-clear' had sounded, Grace regained consciousness to find herself being pulled out of the rubble by a pair of strong hands. When she was back above ground and had wiped the thick dust from her eyes, she found that the hands belonged to an air-raid warden, who was smiling at her and asking if she was alright. She scrutinised his face which looked familiar to her. Then, to her horror, she realised that it was the same man in the white tin hat whom she had glimpsed in Mrs Prentice's' mirror as a young woman. When she asked where her mother was, the warden solemnly shook his head and gently broke the news that she had been crushed by a beam in the explosion and was dead.

As with many supernatural folklore tales, I took this yarn with a pinch of salt – until a couple of years ago, that is, when I read an intriguing manuscript in the main branch of the New York public library. The author was Bridget Hitler, the sister-in-law of the infamous German dictator.

In the manuscript, Bridget, an Irish woman who was married to Adolf Hitler's half brother, Alois, states that, in November 1912, twenty-three-year-old Adolf, at that time a down-and-out, turned up unexpectedly at Lime Street Station, where Bridget and Alois were expecting to meet Anton Roubel, a relative of Alois. But Adolf arrived in his place, admitting that he had made the journey in order to avoid being drafted into the German army. Alois and Bridget gave him refuge in their home at 102 Upper Stanhope Street, in Liverpool's south end. At this time, the area was a magnet for German immigrants seeking work.

Young Adolf spent most of his time in Liverpool wandering around the city, particularly the Pier Head and, as he was something of a painter, he often visited the Walker Art Gallery. However, as time went by and he contributed nothing to the household, he soon wore out his welcome as a lodger and Alois accused him of being a work-shy layabout. When he had first arrived, Bridget had tried to teach him to speak English but she very quickly tired of his superior attitude, so he was left to his own devices once more. There was one person recorded in the manuscript who got on extremely well with Adolf – a Mrs Prentice – who was said to be a neighbour of Bridget's.

Mrs Prentice is described as an astrologer, who gave tarot card readings to anyone interested in having their fortune told. Adolf was apparently fascinated by Mrs Prentice's talents and, in the manuscript, Bridget Hitler writes that, in her opinion, Mrs Prentice converted Adolf into an ardent believer in astrology.

THE INCORRUPTIBLE

In January 1868, about fifty workmen were drafted in to dig up two thousand bodies from a part of St Peter's graveyard in Liverpool's Church Street. Some of the coffins dated as far back as 1707. All the bodies were removed with the utmost decency and propriety and were re-interred in Anfield Cemetery. One particular coffin, which dated from the 1830s, was in an especially poor condition and was so damaged that it split open as it was being transported on to a cart. To the disbelief of the workmen, a fleshy body fell out. A murder enquiry was almost launched due to the fresh state of the suspicious body, which fell out of the crumbling coffin showing no signs whatsoever of decomposition.

The corpse was that of a beautiful woman with long black hair, who seemed to have been in her mid-twenties at the time of her death. There was no rigor mortis evident and a doctor was enlisted to discover why such a fresh corpse was in a coffin which was almost 170 years old. The doctor deduced that it was an example of a poorly-understood phenomenon called incorruptibility – a peculiar state in which the human body refuses to decompose after death. Many saints were incorruptibles, including St Bernadette of Lourdes, who looks as fresh and lifelike today as at the hour when she lay dying in 1879.

The mystery deepened when the name of the incorruptible woman was traced in the parish records. Her name had been Mary Edwards, a twenty-seven-year-old woman who had drowned in the Mersey around 1830. Research into rumours abounding at the time, revealed a very interesting tale. Apparently Mary had been having an affair with a furniture maker by the name of Craven and the poor woman had allegedly been pushed into the river by him when she claimed to be carrying his child.

Mary Edwards' mother Edna, a woman of Romany descent, had had her suspicions regarding her daughter's death. After the funeral, she had burst into a public house where Craven was drinking, walked up to Craven and announced coldly, in full view of the pub, "My daughter Mary is lying in her grave, but she shall not lie fallow and perish. I curse the man who killed my Mary to rot away as he breathes."

Fascinatingly, over the next couple of months, Craven's health started to deteriorate rapidly. His eyes became sunken, his teeth literally fell out and he started to give off a terrible, sour-smelling odour, even though he washed everyday in a desperate attempt to rid himself of the awful stench. His hair had started to detached from his scalp in large clumps and he lost so much weight that he soon resembled a walking skeleton. Some said that just before he died, he confessed to killing Mary Edwards.

Did Craven die of some poorly-understood wasting disease, or was Edna Edwards' sinister curse responsible?

PHANTOM AIRSHIPS

The silent heavens have goings-on.
Wordsworth

From 1909 to 1913, an armada of unidentified airships was seen in the skies above England. The first of these strange sightings occurred on 25 March 1909, in the town of Peterborough. PC Kettle, a Cambridgeshire policeman, was patrolling Cromwell Road in the early hours of the morning, when he heard what he assumed to be the engine of an approaching motor car. As he continued on his beat, he noticed that the sound of the car had changed in pitch to a low buzzing noise, which now seemed to be coming from overhead. Looking skywards, Kettle was blinded by a dazzling light attached to some massive craft, which was blocking out the stars.

The policeman could see that the silhouette was rectangular, and he watched in awe as the craft suddenly accelerated across the starry sky in a southerly direction. Within a minute, the aerial light went out and the mystery airship was lost to sight. PC Kettle returned to his station and gave an account of the strange sighting to his superiors. He was not taken seriously and, instead, was ordered to take a couple of weeks' leave.

More nocturnal flights of strange aerofoils were reported across the land from Liverpool to Kent as the months went by and the newspapers were quick to nickname the epidemic of reports, 'airshipitis'. The aviation experts of the day initially dismissed the 'scareships' as collective hallucinations, despite the fact that these 'imaginary' invaders of English airspace were seen over towns situated hundreds of miles apart. In the summer of 1909, the debunkers had a difficult job explaining away an unidentified airship which actually landed in London.

On the night of 13 May, a Mr Grahame and Mr Bond were strolling across Ham Common on the southwest outskirts of London when they noticed an unusual, cigar-shaped craft, approximately 250 feet in length, hovering about 12 feet above the ground. Grahame and Bond cautiously approached the awesome spectacle.

At close quarters, the two men could make out a couple of silhouetted people moving about in what looked like a gondola suspended beneath the underbelly of the craft. When they were 30 feet from the airship, the beam of a blinding searchlight shone from the gondola and swept the common, singling out the two Londoners. Grahame and Bond stood rooted to the spot as two shadowy figures alighted from the flying machine and came over to meet them. One was a clean-shaven young man who greeted them with an American accent. The other occupant of the Zeppelin-like craft was a German, who asked for some tobacco. Mr Grahame produced a pouch of tobacco and handed it to the German, who held a calabash pipe in his hand. The German took some tobacco from the pouch, handed it back to Mr Grahame, then turned and headed back to the airship, followed closely by his companion.

The American then climbed into a cage-like enclosure in the gondola and began to operate a series of levers that resembled draught beer pump handles. The German sat down behind his associate and began to study a large map dotted with coloured pins. The American pulled one of the levers down extinguishing the brilliant searchlight. The airship started to buzz, then gently rose into the night sky without either of the sinister aeronauts saying goodbye. The unidentified craft raced through the air in a north easterly direction across Richmond Park, towards central London, at an estimated unheard of speed of around 80 miles per hour.

Grahame and Bond informed the authorities, but their story was dismissed as nonsense and the staid editor of *The Times* refused to print an account of the Ham Common encounter, because he also thought that the story was preposterous. The French airships of the day were having difficulty achieving 30mph and the prototype German Zeppelins, hindered by poor aerodynamic design, could not surpass a 35mph limit. So who was the genius behind the unidentified airship that touched down in London?

Four years later, on the evening of 6 January 1913, a large unidentified cigar-shaped airship was seen flying towards the coast of England near the port of Dover. Later that week, a dark cylindrical craft with lights on, was seen flying over the Bristol Channel. The same, mysterious, ghost-like airship was spotted a few nights later by a couple of Welsh policemen in the county of Glamorganshire.

But the airship gave its most peculiar performance in the skies over Liverpool on the Saturday night of 28 January 1913. Thousands of late-night revellers looked up to see the gigantic silent craft, silhouetted against the clear, starry sky. Many of the spectators began to panic at the sight of the stranger in the sky and wondered if it was some foreign airship on a mission to drop bombs on the city. No doubt there were some members of the public who had read *The World Set Free*, HG Wells' prophetic tale of a terrible aerial bombardment from just such a flying machine.

As the citizens looked on, a blinding beam of light shone down on the city from the airship, almost turning night into day. The beam swept across the length of the docks, then turned inland across the city centre as the awestruck public gasped in unison. The immense spotlight settled on the railway network at Edge Hill, then flitted back and forth across Liverpool, focusing occasionally on various landmarks. The searchlight then blinked out and the aircraft headed north and away from the airspace over the city, leaving behind a mystery that has never been solved.

Who were the sinister aeronauts who flew across the nation? The finger of suspicion pointed at Germany, but the zeppelins bore no resemblance to the giant airship which buzzed over the skies of England. One modern explanation is that they were UFOs, perhaps on some reconnaissance programme disguised as dirigibles, so as not to alarm the local terrestrials, or interfere with their cultural beliefs. The extra-terrestrial hypothesis seems far-fetched, but it would at least make some sense of the phenomenon.

MYSTERIOUS MAID

The following strange tale was told to me by my grandmother, Rose Slemen, when I was a child. I have heard many versions of it since and have also read an account of the story written by the distinguished crime historian, Richard Whittington Egan.

In March 1830, a young woman applied for the job of maidservant at a house in Islington Square, Liverpool. Her application was accepted, for although she was dressed rather shabbily, she had an honest and likeable face. Her name was Hannah Brade. Hannah's employer – a widow who lived with her only daughter and young son – initially assumed that the girl was from the lower classes but, on many occasions during the maidservant's two years of service in the household, she was surprised by her often unusual and refined behaviour.

Whenever strangers visited the house, Hannah would become very nervous, as if dreading the arrival of someone she did not wish to meet. As soon as the maid had reassured herself that the visitors were no threat to her and did not recognise her for who she really was, she would go about her business with her usual confidence.

Sometimes the mask slipped. One day the widow and her children returned home from a day out much earlier than expected and were intrigued to hear the lilting strains of Beethoven's Moonlight Sonata coming from the house. It turned out to be Hannah, sitting at the piano in the drawing room. When she suddenly noticed the widow and her children looking on in amazement, she stopped playing immediately and started dusting the ivory keys, flushed with embarrassment. When questioned about her obvious musical talent, Hannah skilfully managed to steer the conversation away from the subject.

The mysterious maid also refused to reveal how she had acquired her knowledge of medicine when she successfully treated the widow's son, when he went down with a serious fever. Within days he made a full recovery. The family doctor – who had warned the widow to expect the worst – was mystified by the boy's sudden return to health and was curious to learn the details of Hannah's top-secret remedy.

On another occasion, the widow's daughter found Hannah's exquisitely-executed pencil sketch of a rustic cottage, crumpled up in a bin. There seemed to be no end to the girl's talents and achievements. Another, even more startling accomplishment, was her command of several foreign languages. One day, at a market in the town, a German was asking for directions in broken English. Hannah, thinking her employer was out of earshot, began to converse fluently with the man in his native tongue. She was also heard singing away happily in French one morning, whilst cooking breakfast.

Hannah soon became the talk of the town. Who was she? and who was she hiding from? She was obviously from a high-class background, for how else could she have acquired such a comprehensive education? Was she perhaps hiding from justice because she had committed a crime? There were so many questions, but alas, no one ever managed to supply the answers.

One morning, the widow was saddened to discover that Hannah had packed up in the night and left the household. Everyone with whom the girl had come into contact missed her tremendously, especially the widow's children, who were literally heart-broken by the maid's departure.

Then, two months later, a mysterious package arrived at the widow's home, containing a number of expensive gifts. They were from Hannah. From that day on, no one heard from Hannah Brade again and today, the questions remain unanswered; who was she? and why did she temporarily assume the guise of a maid-servant?

Was she merely a young woman from the upper echelons of society, sampling the life of the working class? To spend two years seeing how the other half lives would surely be a feat of stoical endurance for a young girl accustomed to the luxuries of the upper classes.

Sadly, we will probably never know why such a beautiful and educated young woman found it necessary to hide behind the apron of a maid-servant.

MERSEYSIDE TIME SLIPS

"Scientific people," said the Time Traveller, "know very well that time is only a kind of space."
HG Wells, *The Time Machine*

Time is the perfect murderer. Every day it indiscriminately extinguishes the lives of around 40,000 individuals worldwide. Rich and poor, black and white – all succumb to time's insidious erosion of their bodies and minds and it seems as if there is not a thing we can do to stop its merciless onslaught. People often talk of killing time, but ironically it is the other way round. If only it were possible to hinder the passage of time, then we could extend our transient lifespans. The Roman writer, Horace, succinctly summed up our mortal predicament in one sentence, over a thousand years ago: "Life's short span forbids us embarking on far-reaching hopes."

To stop the clock and live indefinitely has been a recurring dream throughout the history of mankind, but will the fantasy ever become a reality? It is my belief that the flow of time can be controlled and that, incredible as it seems, various individuals have inadvertently moved backwards and forwards through the 'fourth dimension' – the official scientific description of time. These time-walkers will be examined in this chapter, but first let us take a cursory look at the nature of time from a scientific viewpoint.

What we call time is still something of a mystery. Until the German mathematical physicist Albert Einstein (1979-1955) came along, scientists regarded time as an absolute, universal, unchanging something, which flowed steadily on in one direction, like a mighty river, from the past to the future. Einstein proved that this was simply not the case. Long before experiments verified that his reasoning was correct, Einstein told the sceptical scientific community of his day that time was elastic, reversible and actually ran at different rates in different areas of the universe, which made a mockery of the traditional notions of time laid down by the English scientist and mathematician, Sir Isaac Newton (1642-1727).

Einstein's claim was regarded as being revolutionary, even nonsensical initially: objects which are moving, age more slowly than stationary objects. As an example, imagine a set of identical twins. One of them climbs aboard a rocket which takes off from Earth and begins a five-year space voyage at a speed very close to light's velocity (which is 186, 281 miles per second). By the time that astronaut returns to Earth, he would find that his terrestrial twin is now 50 years older than him!

Einstein's incredible theory of time dilation has now been proved in many ways. If we had two, highly-accurate, atomic clocks and we placed one at an airport and one in Concorde and flew it to New York and back, we would find that the readouts from the two clocks would be different when they were subsequently compared, because the clock on Concorde would have ticked more slowly than the stationary clock in the airport. Time dilation has also been observed in sub-atomic particles such as the muon, which decays on average after 2.2 microseconds.

These particles are created when cosmic rays enter the upper atmosphere and are so short-lived that, in theory, they ought not to persist for long enough to reach the Earth's surface, but they do, because they are moving so fast that their time-scale, relative to ours, is slowed down.

If you are still not convinced that there is more to time than meets the eye, you should go out on a cloudless, moonless night and look up at the stars; you will be participating in a type of time-travel yourself, because you will be seeing the stars as they were many millions of years ago. If you see a faint frizzy patch of luminosity to the upper left of the Pegasus Constellation, you will be looking at the Andromeda Galaxy, which is the nearest galaxy to ours. But you will not be seeing this galaxy as it is, but as it was 2.2 million years ago, because it is so far away, that the light emitted from it takes that length of time to reach your eyes here on Earth. In other words, we are looking back into the remote past when we look up into the sky.

Astronomers recently announced that a cluster of galaxies known as Abell 2065 had been discovered in the Corona Borealis Constellation, a billion light years away, and the light from these remote stellar objects had started its journey to their telescopes around the time mankind was beginning to evolve from the primordial sludge on Earth.

BOLD STREET TIME WARP

The following story is an account of a man who inadvertently strolled into the past early in July 1996 in Liverpool city centre. Frank, an off-duty policeman from Melling and his wife, Carol, were in Liverpool shopping one Saturday afternoon. At Central Station, they split up; Carol set off to what was then Dillons Bookshop in Bold Street to buy a copy of Irvine Welsh's book, *Trainspotting*, while Frank headed for a record store in Ranelagh Street, to look for a CD. About twenty minutes later, he was walking up the incline near the Lyceum, which emerges in Bold Street, intending to meet Carol in the bookshop, when he suddenly noticed that he had somehow entered an oasis of quiet.

Suddenly, a small box-shaped van, like something out of the 1950s, sped across his path, sounding its horn as it narrowly missed him. Frank noted that the van had the name 'Caplan's' emblazoned on its side. When he looked down at the ground, he noticed that he was standing in the road. He immediately thought this was strange, because the bottom of Bold Street was pedestrianised.

Frank crossed the road and was immediately struck by

the fact that Dillons bookshop was no longer there. In its place, stood a store with the name 'Cripps' over its two entrances. Confused, he peered into the window of Cripps and found no books on display. They had been replaced by a large collection of women's handbags and shoes.

The policeman scanned the street and saw that the people were wearing clothes that would have been worn in the 1940s and 50s, which really unnerved him. He realised that he had somehow walked into the Bold Street of forty-odd years ago. Frank then caught sight of a girl of about twenty, dressed in the clothes of the mid-1990s – hipsters and a lime-coloured sleeveless top – and he breathed a sigh of relief. The bag she carried had the name Miss Selfridge on it, which helped to reassure him that he was still somehow partly in 1996, but the paradox remained. He smiled at the girl as she walked past him and entered Cripps. As he followed her through the entrance, the building's interior changed in a flash back to Dillons bookshop. He was back in his own time. Without considering his actions, he grabbed the girl by the arm.

"Did you see that?" he asked her.

"Yeah. I thought it was a new shop that had just opened. I was going in to look at the clothes, but it's a bookshop," she said, calmly.

She then just laughed, shook her head and walked back out again. Frank later described how the girl had looked back and shaken her head again in disbelief. When he told his wife about the incident, she said that she had not noticed anything strange, but Frank was adamant that he had not hallucinated the episode.

I gave an account of this strange timeslip on the *Billy Butler Show*. Within minutes, people were ringing in to the station to confirm that, in the late 1950s and early 1960s, there had been a store called Cripps, situated in the exact location where Dillons bookshop now stood; there had also been a local firm called Caplan's in existence around the same time. What's more, I also received letters and telephone calls from listeners who had also experienced strange things in the same part of Bold Street where the policeman had stepped into another era.

A man who worked on the renovation of the Lyceum building in Bold Street, said that his digital watch went backwards for two hours one day. On another occasion, he put down his safety helmet and when he looked down, literally seconds later, it had vanished, yet no one was within fifty feet of him.

THE SAD SPECTRE
OF SMITHDOWN ROAD

The following spooky incident happened in Liverpool in the early 1990s and was even reported in the *Liverpool Echo*.

One morning at around four o'clock, twenty-four year-old Alan was walking home from a pub in Smithdown Road. There had been a stay-behind because the landlady was celebrating her recent engagement, and Alan felt quite drunk. He was walking near Sefton General Hospital, on Smithdown Road, when he noticed a girl standing near a bus stop. She wore an incredibly short dress with a revealing top and had long blonde hair. She looked about nineteen or twenty and Alan assumed she was waiting for a taxi. She just stood there shivering, stamping her high heels because of the cold. "You're not on the game are you?" Alan joked, attempting to chat her up.

The girl smiled and shook her head.

"I'm dead cold," she complained.

Alan saw his opportunity and took off his denim jacket and offered it to her. "Who said chivalry was dead?" he laughed as the girl put it on. Three sizes too large, it looked ridiculous on her. "Waiting for a taxi?" he asked.

"No … waiting for my boyfriend," she replied, looking down Smithdown Road for any sign of him.

Alan's heart sank. He thought, "Just my luck. She's already going out with someone."

"He does my head in, you know… I've been waiting here for ages. He always does this," added the girl.

"Does what?"

"Says he's gonna pick me up and then doesn't turn up."

"Get another boyfriend who's more reliable then," Alan said, giving her a wink.

"Nah, I love Tony," she answered smiling.

"Ah, but does he love you?" asked Alan cheekily.

"Oh, I bet he's not coming," moaned the girl, looking worried. "I hope nothing's happened to him."

"No, he's probably with some girl. We fellas are only human y'know, despite our alien appearance," laughed Alan, trying to cheer her up.

The girl tutted and walked along. Alan walked with her, admiring her long elegant legs and beautiful figure. She was a real stunner. "What's your name?" he asked.

"Jodie," she replied.

"Ooh, Jodie Foster eh? My name's Alan. My mates call me Alan Ladd."

Jodie smiled and walked on. Then she suddenly bowed her head as if she was going to cry and ran into Toxteth Park Cemetery. Alan thought she was either going to be sick, or that she was going to 'powder her nose'. He wanted to relieve himself too, after all the drinking.

After about ten minutes, Alan shouted into the darkness of the cemetery, "Jodie! Jodie? Are you okay?" As he crept past the gravestones, there was no sign of her. He half expected to find her on the ground, out cold with drink, yet she had not appeared drunk. By now it was almost dawn and the sky was getting paler by the minute. "You had me worried there girl," he called out aloud as he thought he saw her, but it was just his denim jacket, draped over a gravestone. "What's she playing at?" he mumbled. Then he saw Jodie's face, on the gravestone. A photograph of her to be precise and, underneath it, an inscription saying that she had been born in 1970 and had died tragically in 1990, just six months earlier!

Alan was terrified by now. He ran out of the cemetery into Smithdown Road and did not stop running until he reached his home almost a mile away. He fell down on his doorstep when he got home and with a trembling hand inserted the key in the Yale lock.

A week later, he told his two best friends about the ghost he had tried to chat up and Brian, one of his mates, recalled that his sister had been a friend of Jodie's. Brian then told the sad story. Jodie had arranged to meet her boyfriend near the bus stop at Sefton General Hospital on Smithdown Road. She had been unaware that she had a hole in her heart and she collapsed and died. Although people tried to help by taking her to the hospital, there was nothing that anyone could do. Jodie's parents phoned her boyfriend and told him the bad news, he was so inconsolable that he vowed never to drive up Smithdown Road again and has never done so to this day.

On the following night, Alan and Brian visited Jodie's grave and placed a bouquet of carnations on it, because Brian's sister had said carnations that had been her favourite flowers. As the lads walked away from the cemetery, Alan glanced back and was certain he saw Jodie waving. Her ghost is still occasionally seen by motorists driving up Smithdown Road in the early hours of the morning. As recently as 1996, a taxi driver stopped for the girl at three in the morning and when he looked again, the pavement was deserted.

RINGS ON HER FINGERS

The following spooky tale is one of the earliest recorded ghost stories in the North West and allegedly took place in Liverpool in the autumn of 1826.

In October of that year, fifty-six-year-old Liverpool pawnbroker William Poole buried his wife Rose, who had died from typhoid. His neighbours, who lived in a lane off Dale Street, thought it was disgraceful that he was already flirting with young women in the local tavern, so soon after his wife's death. Only a fortnight after the funeral, Poole was already seriously involved with a pretty young girl called Katie Holland. Katie was only seventeen and had just broken up with her boyfriend, so she sought solace in the arms of the lecherous pawnbroker.

By the end of November, Katie discovered she was pregnant with Poole's child and so the couple married a week later at St George's Church, which once stood in Derby Square. Poole was having quite a hard time financially and was concerned that he might not be able to afford a decent wedding ring for his bride. However, on the day of the wedding, a fabulous thick gold band, encrusted with a sparkling array of sapphires and rubies was put on Katie's finger. Later, when the couple were honeymooning in North Wales, Mr Poole bestowed five other breathtaking gold rings upon his beautiful young bride.

After a fortnight, the newly-married couple returned to Liverpool and Poole carried Katie over the threshold of his house and up four flights of stairs to the four poster bed. They were tired from the long journey and soon fell asleep.

About four o'clock in the morning, Katie awoke and saw moonlight shining through the bedroom window. She closed her eyes and stretched out her left arm but as she did so, she felt icy cold fingers grasping her outstretched hand. She glanced sideways and was horrified to see a woman dressed in what seemed to be a white shroud. The woman looked as if she was dead. A thin layer of bluish-white skin lightly covered her skeletal face. Katie noted that the ghoul's dark, prominent eyes were filled with sadness as she fought to free her hand. Katie tried to scream but her throat had closed up with fear. Then the corpse-like woman suddenly muttered, "Give me my rings back ... give me them!" as her bony fingers tried to pull off the wedding ring and the so-called friendship rings.

Katie suddenly managed to let out a scream that startled her husband from his slumber. Katie told William about the gruesome apparition and she insisted on sleeping with lit candles placed about the room.

The following afternoon, while William was at work, Katie was alone in the house. She was washing clothes in the kitchen, when she heard a whining sound behind her. She turned around and saw the same ghoulish figure standing in the hall with its arms outstretched coming towards her. The figure was whimpering and pleading, "Please give me my rings back."

Katie shot out of the back door and into the arms of the Reverend Richard Kelly, the clergyman who had married her and William. Having listened to her account of the haunting, the vicar took Katie to his house, which was annexed to St George's Church and gave her a drink to steady her. After some moments of contemplation, he suddenly stood up and said, "I hope I'm wrong. Come with me," and he led Katie out into the churchyard. He threaded his way through the gravestones until he came to the grave of Poole's deceased wife, Rose. The grave had obviously been disturbed, so the Reverend summoned two burly grave-diggers to exhume her body. As they opened the coffin Katie fainted when she noticed that the decomposing corpse was identical to the ghost in the shroud which had visited her twice. Furthermore, the rings were missing from the hands of the corpse.

When William Poole was confronted by the Reverend Kelly, he broke down and admitted having desecrated the grave and stolen the rings from his dead wife in order to give them to his new bride. On hearing this, Katie removed the loathsome rings and flung them at her despicable husband. Even after he had returned the rings to his wife's coffin she could no longer bear to look at him and soon abandoned him.

Ironically, a year later, two grave-robbers, Robert Tryer and John Woods ransacked the grave of Rose Poole and stole her rings and jewellery. Although they were captured and transported to Australia, the rings of Rose Poole were never found. There were rumours that they were purchased by a family with the all too common surname Jones. Perhaps the tainted rings are still being passed down through the generations to their unwitting descendants.

ASHES TO ASHES

In 1985, seventy-six-year-old Maud lost her husband Bill when he died of cancer. The couple, who lived in the Merseyside area, were inseparable and Bill knew that when he died, Maud would feel utterly lost. During the couple's last conversation, Maud said that life without him would be unbearable. "Keep your chin up love," said Bill, "because if there is a life after this one, I'll be there looking over you night and day. When the worst happens, just carry on and pretend I'm in the room with you. Call me by my old familiar name."

Bill was cremated and Maud kept his ashes in an ornamental urn which she kept by her bed. Each night, before she switched off the light, she would say goodnight to the urn. She knew it was silly, but it was her way of coping with life without Bill.

In the Christmas of 1985, Maud went into town to do some shopping. In one of the large department stores she went to the ladies toilet. Instead of hanging her handbag on a hook, she unwisely put it on the floor. Within seconds, someone had reached under the door and snatched her bag, which contained her pension book, four hundred pounds in cash that she had saved to buy her grandchildren Christmas presents, her late husband's wallet and wedding ring, and a cash card along with her PIN number, which she had foolishly scrawled on a piece of paper because she never could remember the four-digit code.

Maud reported the theft to the manager of the store and the police, who gave her a lift home in a squad car. Because she did not have her keys, a little boy in the street had to go through the bathroom window to open the door for her. She went upstairs to the bedroom and cradled the urn containing Bill's ashes, sobbing inconsolably. "Oh, Bill. How could someone do this to me? Help me Bill," she wept.

The following morning the phone rang, and Maud answered it. It was the manager of the department store. He said that the handbag had been found intact and it seemed that nothing was missing. She only had to collect and sign for the handbag. What's more, the manager said he would give Maud a free Christmas hamper because of the trauma she had been through.

Maud was elated. She used the money a sympathetic neighbour had given her to take a taxi to the store, but when she arrived the manager was baffled. "I didn't call you and no one has reported finding your handbag. Someone must be pulling your leg. I'm terribly sorry."

"But how would they know my telephone number?" said Maud with a sinking feeling.

"Oh dear!" said the manager as he looked at Maud, "I hope I'm wrong, but the person who phoned you could be the one who stole your bag. Perhaps he told you to come here just to get you out of the house so he and his associates could empty it, because I assume they have the keys. I don't want to frighten you, but they were probably watching you as you left the house."

"Oh no!" Maud cried, starting to shake. The manager ran to the nearest phone and alerted the police. By the time they got to the house, the robbers had already been and had stripped out everything of value: jewellery, the video, the television, everything that was worth something was gone, even the phone. Maud was led into the bedroom to see the mess the robbers had left. Of course, the first thing she looked for was Bill's urn. It was gone. This was the last straw; she felt faint and collapsed on to the bed. An ambulance was called and she was taken to hospital with high blood pressure and reoccurring dizzy spells.

Maud woke up several times during the night feeling more alone than she had ever felt in her life. At around three in the morning, she opened her eyes to see Bill standing at the foot of the bed. He was surrounded by a silvery light and was smiling at her.

"Bill, is that you?" Maud gasped, stretching out her hands to the vision of her late husband.

"Yes dear, everything's going to be just fine. Go to sleep now. Everything will be okay in the morning, you just go to sleep," said Bill calmly.

"But Bill, you're …" Maud stammered, unable to finish the sentence.

"I know, but I'm waiting somewhere very near and I still feel very much alive. I gave those cowards who took your bag quite a scare. Now go to sleep, love. You need rest," he told her and started to fade away. Suddenly, there was no one at the foot of the bed anymore, but he left behind an aura of peace and tranquillity. Maud's eyelids felt heavy and she was soon sleeping soundly.

At ten in the morning, two policemen called into the ward bringing strange news. The criminals who had taken her handbag and robbed her house were a woman named Jackie and her boyfriend Giles. They had confessed to the robbery and the housebreaking after receiving an unpleasant shock.

Giles had opened the burial urn and was peering into it with his girlfriend and laughing, when some of the ashes shot out and burnt Giles in the eyes. Jackie repeatedly bathed his eyes, but he still could not see. In the end, she took him to casualty where the doctors asked him how he got the ash in his eyes. Giles was in so much agony that his guard dropped and he made a confession, telling the medical staff the whole heinous story. The police were called in and the couple were formally charged.

Maud remembered the vision of her husband in the wee small hours and how he had promised her that everything would be fine. The incident was investigated by the Psychical Research Society and, as is usual in these cases, the whole episode was filed away for posterity. It took three months for the robber's eyesight to return and an ophthalmologist who treated him said he could not explain the blindness.

Maud was later reunited with the precious urn and still talks to it on a regular basis.

A MARRIAGE MADE IN HELL

The following story allegedly happened in Liverpool in the 1960s. There are many fanciful versions of the tale that have been circulating in the city for many years but this is the original and tells the story of a young girl who was forever dreaming about marriage.

In the mid-1960s Liverpool, a young woman named Collette worked in a textile factory near Wood Street in the city centre. She was a pretty but introverted girl, who had no real friends at the factory. She kept to herself and hardly ever spoke to the eight other women who worked with her.

Each day at lunch, the factory girls would go to a cafe in Bold Street but Collette never went with them. Instead, she bought cigarettes from a kiosk round the corner and then walked up Bold Street, window shopping. She always seemed to be in a world of her own. Every day, she would gaze through the window of a certain shop that had expensive wedding dresses on display and she spent almost all of her lunch-hour staring dreamily at these dresses. Chrissy, one of her workmates, used to watch her and wonder what the lonely girl was thinking of.

Collette kept a diary of all of her most intimate thoughts, fantasising over various film stars and wondering what type of man her future husband would be. She always imagined he would be tall, dark and very handsome. Collette was attractive but seemed to have difficulty meeting the opposite sex. One night at her flat in Huskisson Street, her old neighbour Mona heard her sobbing. She tapped on her door and asked if she was okay. Collette came to the door in a dreadful state and Mona took her down to her basement flat and gave her a cup of tea. Collette said she had asked a boy out and he had turned her down. Mona said he must have been a fool and tried to boosted her confidence by saying how pretty she was and that boys were ten-a-penny.

About an hour later, as Collette left Mona's flat, she met a sinister old man on the stairs who had only just moved into the flats. He always dressed in black and was always accompanied by a black cat. She only knew him as Mr Rose

"Hello, Mr Rose," she said, guardedly.

"If we meet on the stairs, we'll never meet in heaven," said Mr Rose, with a snigger. Then in a serious tone he added, "Collette, I couldn't help overhearing you and Mona before."

"Yes?" exclaimed Collette, beginning to blush.

"I think I can help you. Come on," and he beckoned her to come into his flat. Collette felt very nervous, and the old man's flat was very dark, with dusty old books on astrology and the occult everywhere and a crystal ball on the table. He told her to sit at a table and handed her a piece of paper.

"That's a pact with the Devil," he explained in a matter-of-fact way and offered her a pen.

Collette grinned and examined the words scrawled on the paper. They seemed to be in Latin and were so small, she could not make head nor tail of them. "What does it say?" she asked.

"In return for your soul, you can have anything you desire. Just sign your name at the bottom of the page," said Mr Rose, uncapping an old fountain pen and handed it to her.

"I don't believe in all that stuff about the Devil."

"I know, yes," said Mr Rose, "but just sign it anyway, go on."

"But …" stammered the girl.

"No buts. Just do it! Do it! Go on. You know you want to," said the old man, fixing her with a hypnotic stare.

Collette found herself signing it, "I want to marry a man who's tall dark and handsome," she wished out loud, then left the room, giggling and trotted upstairs to her flat.

On the following day, during her lunchbreak, Collette was gazing in the shop window again, focusing on a beautiful satin and lace wedding gown, when suddenly she saw a face reflected in the window: a tall dark-haired man with a handsome face. He was looking over her shoulder and his sudden presence naturally startled the girl.

"Oooh! Who are you?" she exclaimed.

As she looked at the man, he grinned and he looked so dashing, but the pupils of his eyes suddenly burned with a dim red light. Collette stumbled back in fear against the window. The figure then glided towards her. "Don't be afraid, Collette. I want to marry you. I want you. You made your promise to me," said the weird stranger. Collette let out a scream and fled up Bold Street in a state of terror. When she got home she barricaded herself into her flat and hid under a table. At eight that night, the stranger called at her house. Collette looked through the window and saw that he was holding a brown paper parcel. "Don't let him in!" she screamed, but Mona had already ushered him inside. He tapped on Collette's door, saying, "Let me in, Collette,. I love you. I'm your future husband," then suddenly turned nasty, shouting, "Let me in, damn you!"

Then there was silence. Collette sat up all night drinking coffee and listening to her radio. As soon as morning came, she planned to leave her flat for good and started writing down all the strange events in her diary. However, she never got to finish her entry, because she dropped dead of a massive heart attack.

Mona found the girl the next day with her eyes wide open, filled with terror. When the police arrived, they saw that someone had left a brown-paper parcel on the landing outside the girl's flat. It contained a black silk and satin wedding dress, a dark replica of the one in the window in Bold Street. When Mona read the dead girl's diary, she shuddered and decided to confront old Mr Rose, but his flat was completely empty. Nobody had seen him leave and nobody ever saw that old man again.

SPOOKY JUKEBOX

The following story may seem far-fetched, but it was reported in local newspapers and featured on a local BBC news programme.

In the mid-1980s, an electrician was trying to fix a troublesome jukebox at a pub in northern Liverpool, when he accidentally touched the live circuit board and suffered a fatal heart attack. The barmaid, Lorraine, let out a scream when she saw the electrician collapse and was deeply shaken by the tragedy. Around a fortnight after his death, weird things started to occur in the pub, all centred round the jukebox. A lorry driver went in one lunchtime for a pint and a pie and went over to the jukebox and keyed in a Bruce Springsteen song, 'Dancin' in the Dark'. Instead, the jukebox played 'Heat of the Moment' by a band called Asia.

Three hours later, the lorry driver was burned alive when his HGV, which was carrying tons of vegetable oil, jackknifed near Knutsford, hit the central reservation and burst into flames. One of the drinkers who heard the news on the pub radio was the first to connect the subject of the jukebox's song 'Heat of the Moment' and the lorry driver's death, but his mates said it was just a morbid coincidence.

Then a woman named Mary went into the pub one evening and walked up to the jukebox. She pressed the buttons to play Michael Jackson's 'One Day In Your Life' but, instead, a golden oldie, 'Viva Espania' came on and the woman just laughed. The following day her husband won a competition in a magazine – two weeks in Spain for two people. They were both soon holidaying in Benidorm.

That same week, a middle-aged man named Bob went into the pub to play darts with his mates. He went to the jukebox, inserted his money, then selected an old Beatles song. Instead of 'Hey Jude', 'If You Leave Me Now', a song by the American group Chicago began to play. Bob shrugged and went back to his darts. Minutes later, Bob's brother walked in with tears in his eyes, with news that Bob's wife had just been knocked down and killed by a drunken driver.

By now, the regular drinkers in the pub were starting to notice a connection between the songs on the jukebox and the corresponding incidents that were happening to the customers. The drinkers urged the landlady to replace the spooky jukebox, but she just said they were all crazy and there was nothing wrong with it. She put some coins in to prove her point, selecting a song by a favourite group of hers, Pickety Witch. Instead, a song by David Bowie came on, entitled 'Ashes to Ashes', prompting the drinkers to warn the landlady that the pub would probably burn down. There was no fire, but the outcome was much more sinister.

The landlady went to Woolwich in London to see her ex-husband who had been fighting cancer. His common-law wife had been looking after him and she asked her where her ex-husband was. The woman laughed coldly and pointed to an urn containing the man's ashes; he had died a month back and had instructed his partner to have him cremated. The landlady fainted and when she regained consciousness, she accused her ex-husband's partner of being an ignorant, cold-hearted woman and left forthwith.

The landlady immediately had the haunted jukebox removed. According to eight witnesses, including an off-duty policeman, as the unplugged jukebox was being carried into a van, it started to play music for about ten seconds. The song it played was very fitting indeed: it was 'Thank You for the Music' by Abba ...

THE VENGEFUL GRAVE

In the summer of July 1997, a woman named Elaine visited a cemetery in Allerton, Liverpool, to put flowers on her mother's grave, as she did most Sundays. On this particular sunny afternoon, there was an unusual quietness; hardly any traffic passed by on the main road outside and there were only three other people in the cemetery.

The tranquillity was broken when a clod of earth whizzed past Elaine and landed with great force on the ground beside her, missing her head by inches. She looked around, expecting to see a mischievous child but there were none to be seen. She had a little silent talk with her mum and was about to walk away, when a pebble hit the stone urn on her mother's grave. Elaine had just filled the urn with flowers and looked round angrily to find the disrespectful joker.

An elderly woman passed by and Elaine was about to ask her if she had seen any kids throwing things, when another clod of earth came down and hit the woman's leg. They looked at each other, baffled. The pensioner called to her husband who was sitting in a parked car on the path. He came over and soon Elaine and the couple were looking for the culprits. Just then, a handful of gravel showered the car. The old man was furious and stalked off down the grass verge that ran parallel to the row of gravestones. He then saw something that stopped him in his tracks. A clod of earth lifted up off a grave and went hurtling into the air. It thudded on to a marble headstone, sending soil flying everywhere.

The three of them walked over to the grave where the clod had seemingly taken off by itself. The old woman said her husband had probably seen a mole but Elaine was doubtful. Then the three of them looked on in disbelief as a handful of gravel and stones shot up from the grave and landed about twenty-five feet away on the same black marble headstone. Some of the debris again landed on the car, which was close to the marble headstone.

This continued for about fifteen minutes but none of the observers dared to venture close to the grave to get a better look. Then, a middle-aged man approached with a bunch of flowers, saying he was visiting his uncle's grave. He smiled when Elaine and the elderly couple recited their accounts of the stones shooting up off the grave. Without being told which grave they were referring to, the man casually walked over to the weather-beaten white headstone and said, "This is the grave, isn't it?"

The three other people nodded, amazed at the way the man seemed unafraid of the eerie grave. Then the man told a bizarre story. "This is the grave of a woman who lived in my neighbourhood. She was always fighting with her husband, always having a go at him over something or other. The police were forever being called out whenever she kicked off. Her husband was terrified of her because she tried to knife him once. She used to throw plates and all sorts at him, but when she died in a car crash, he was devastated. He told me he really loved her, even though they were always fighting."

The man then walked back towards the three onlookers. He pointed to the black marble grave that had been the target of the phantom missile-thrower and said, "That's where her hen-pecked husband was buried. He died from cancer a couple of years ago. He was supposed to be buried in his wife's grave but his brother arranged for him to be buried there instead. You know what families are like!"

As the man explained all this, another pebble hit the black marble grave. Elaine and the elderly couple jumped with fright but the man just laughed and turned to face the white marble headstone, saying, "Stop it, Margie. Rest in peace, girl."

Within seconds, the elderly couple were in their car. They let Elaine get in with them and the car screeched and sped off down the avenue outside the cemetery, leaving behind the brave man to tend to his uncle's grave.

FATAL INFATUATION

A certain department store now covers the forgotten little cemetery of Church Alley, off Liverpool's Church Street. Thousands of shoppers stroll along this bustling thoroughfare quite unaware that, in their vicinity, the remains of Richard Worthington lie in the cold earth and have done so for one hundred and fifty years. His ghost is said to haunt the department store that now stands on his unmarked grave. In 1977, a psychic who knew nothing of the story I am about to relate, was given permission to investigate the haunting. He said he felt that the spirit was heartbroken and that his surname was Worthing, or Worthington. Perhaps when I tell you Worthington's story, his spirit will at last be able to rest in peace ...

In 1847, nineteen year-old Richard Worthington from Blackburn got a job at a wine merchant's cellar off Lime Street. At around six o'clock one October evening, Richard left the premises and headed for his home near what is now Great Crosshall Street. As he strolled along, the heavens opened and he was lashed by torrential rain. Lightning flashed through the low, oppressive clouds and thunder rolled across the town.

As Richard ran blindly through the downpour, he collided with a girl at St George's Place, near St George's Hall. The impact knocked the girl to the floor. Richard apologised repeatedly and picked her up. The girl was beautiful and spoke with a slight Welsh accent. She said her name was Megan Davies and that her life was in danger. She was saturated and her long, black, curly hair clung to her face. Her big, blue eyes stared timidly up at Richard, who was quite tall. She looked so vulnerable and as he gazed into those child-like eyes it was love at first sight. He took off his coat and wrapped it around the waif-like girl, then escorted her to the little rented house he had recently moved into. He sat her down in front of a blazing fire, gave her a towel and then went upstairs to change into some dry clothes.

As she dried out, Megan told him a sad story. She had come to Liverpool from Anglesey two years ago and had been living with a forty year-old man named Robert for over a year, but had discovered that he was married. After that huge shock, there came two more dreadful discoveries: the first was that he had another wife in Everton and, even more shockingly, he had murdered a third wife in Toxteth and buried her somewhere in Sefton Park.

"How did you come by all this information and why is your life in danger?" Richard asked, pouring her a glass of gin which she downed in one gulp. She trembled and told him that she had found Robert's diary in a chest in the attic and, when he found her reading the book, he chased her with a knife and tried to kill her. However, she escaped and had been on the run from him ever since. She pointed to a small scar on her left breast and said that was where the knife had grazed her during the attack.

"We must go to the police," Richard said angrily. He wondered how some brute could hurt a defenceless girl like Megan. His blood boiled at the thought.

Megan threw cold water on the idea. "We can't, Richard. Robert has friends in the police force and told me that he and the head of the Lancashire police are both freemasons in the same lodge. I fear it won't be long until the police arrest me and kill me on his orders. I'm sick with fear. I will have to flee Lancashire and return to Wales."

She started to cry, "I'm very grateful for the kind help you have shown but I must be on my way," and she headed for the door but Richard would not let her leave, telling her that she should at least lie low in his lodgings for a week or so. He would tell no one, so she would be safe from the evil bigamist and murderer. Megan accepted his offer and, the following day, she practically seduced the wine merchant's assistant as he was bathing in a tub by the fire. Richard had had a strict puritanical upbringing and was uncomfortable at first but gradually became accustomed to sleeping with her each night. The neighbours made much of the fact that the couple were 'living in sin' but he didn't care. He was so in love with Meg and was secretly saving half of his apprentice wages each week to buy her an engagement ring. He had heard people talk about love but now he knew what it was all about; he was totally besotted with his Anglesey girl.

In December of that year, Richard was making his way home with a bottle of wine when he was astonished to see his beloved Meg battling with a tall grey haired man near the top of Dale Street. He was shaking her by the shoulders and had a long-bladed knife in his other hand. The ground was icy, and the stranger and Megan slid about as they grappled with each other. She was screaming at the man, who shouted, "You maniac! Trying to ruin my marriage!"

Richard ran across the icy cobblestones shouting, "Leave her alone!" The stranger let go of Megan and wheeled round. Richard hit him on the head with the bottle of wine. The man buckled to his knees and Megan tried to grab the knife, but the stranger held on to it and her fingers were cut by the blade. A crowd of bystanders then circled the three battling figures. Richard punched the man and tried to grab the knife but the man screamed, "Get away or I'll strike!"

Megan bit the hand that held the knife and the man slapped her face. This enraged Richard. He lunged forward and the stranger lifted his hand in defence. The blade went into Richard's chest, piercing his heart and he fell down on the icy cobbles, reaching out to Megan as his life ebbed away. But she ignored him, instead pleading with the stranger, "Robert! I'm sorry! Please don't desert me for her! I love you Robert! We can go away together!" A brief puzzled frown crossed Richard Worthington's face as he looked at the object of his love, then he quietly died.

He never knew that Megan was an escaped inmate from the mental hospital less than a hundred yards away, near Dawson Street. She had a history of self harming; the knife wound on her breast being one example. She had psychotic tendencies and often became fixated on strangers. After her escape, she had followed a man around for months. She only knew his name was Robert and that he was married and lived in Toxteth. She would habitually sit on his doorstep, claiming he was her husband. When Robert threatened to call the police, she had tried to knife him and that had been the beautiful stalker's intention when she followed him to Dale Street that fateful evening.

Megan Davies was promptly locked away again in a more secure unit and Richard Worthington, the teenager who had been blinded by her beauty, was laid to rest at the cemetery off Church Street.

THE GREEN EYE OF THE MERSEY

On 21 October 1839, the night skies over Cheshire lit up with a blinding blue flash and scores of people saw a meteor fall to earth. The following morning, a farmer near Hollowmoor Heath discovered a small crater in his field. None of the cows would venture near it and the farmer noticed that there was a black object the size of a billiard ball embedded in the centre of the crater. The farmer showed the object to a clergyman and he passed it on to his friend William Ibbotson, who was an amateur astronomer. Ibbotson cleaned the meteorite and sawed it in half. In the middle there was an object so hard, that the saw blade bounced off it. Ibbotson studied the precious stone which was creamy white, like an opal.

The unearthly gemstone was the size of an egg and had a peculiar flaw – it contained a circular emerald-coloured stone which made it resemble a glass eye with a green iris. Ibbotson sent a report of his findings to the Royal Astronomical Society in London but never received a reply and he decided the 'Green Eye' as he called it, would be an unusual birthday gift for his niece who lived in Dublin.

Five months later, Ibbotson boarded the steamer *William Huskisson* at Liverpool Docks but the ship failed to reach Ireland. It is not known why the ship sank in the middle of the Irish Sea, as it was in excellent condition and its captain and crew had made the crossing hundreds of times. Forty passengers, including Mr Ibbotson, perished.

Weeks later, Ibbotson's suitcase was washed up on to the coast of Hoylake and a man named George Peters opened it and found the strange Green Eye stone. After taking it to a jeweller who could not identify it, Peters decided to try and sell it in Liverpool. Twenty-four hours later, however, he died from a typhoid-like fever which claimed fifteen thousand victims in the town. So-called 'fever sheds' were opened at Mount Pleasant and the body of William Peters was literally cast on to a heap of bodies in one of them.

A poor Irishman named John Lorne stripped and searched the plague corpses and came across the Green Eye. Delighted at his lucky find, he showed it to his friends at a pub in Hope Street, saying he intended to get it valued. The landlord was very superstitious and felt it radiated evil and told Lorne to take it off the premises. The Irishman scoffed at the landlord's comments and went home.

Half an hour later, a boy ran into the pub crying that Lorne was dying outside his lodging house in Percy Street, impaled on the railings. Two railings had gone right through his back and were protruding from his chest. He coughed up blood as he gave an account of what had happened. A man had run into his room and demanded the gemstone. There was a struggle, the man pushed Lorne through his open window and he had landed on the railings. Lorne's friends made the fatal mistake of trying to lift their companion off the railings, despite his gut wrenching screams. Their well-meant actions killed Lorne because as they lifted him, one railing severed an artery and the other ruptured his liver.

As he breathed his last, the Green Eye fell out of Lorne's hand. One of the bystanders picked it up and a fight broke out. The dead man's cousin, George Wishart, successfully claimed it and he later emigrated to the Isle of Man. One day, Wishart decided to have the Green Eye mounted in a gold locket, but on his way to the jewellers, he dropped dead in the street. A pathologist said he had died from cardio-congestive failure but could not understand why, as Wishart had a cast-iron constitution.

Wishart's niece, May Allen, took possession of the jinxed gemstone and, within a year, five of her friends had died in tragic accidents. Even so, Mrs Allen refused to believe that the Green Eye was cursed. In December 1909, she decided to visit relatives in Liverpool with her son Ernest. They boarded the steamship *Ellan Vannin* and yes, you've guessed it, that ship sank in mysterious circumstances on its way to the port in Liverpool Bay. Look-outs in the Wirral lighthouse were horrified to see her lights go out, then, within seconds, the ship went under the waves. Everyone on board was drowned and the cause of the sudden sinking has never been determined. The bodies of May and Ernest Allen were buried on the western side of St James's Cemetery, next to the Anglican Cathedral. Relatives of Mrs Allen confirmed that she had taken the Green Eye with her to show to her cousins in Liverpool, but it was not found on her body. We must therefore presume that the cursed Green Eye is lying somewhere at the bottom of the Mersey, probably within the wreck of the *Ellan Vannin* which still lies beneath the waves of Liverpool Bay. Considering its dark history, perhaps the Green Eye of the Mersey should be left where it lies.

A WAGGING TONGUE

The following story, which took place in Liverpool in the seventeenth century, is a tale about the dangers of jumping to conclusions.

In the year 1627, Jeremiah Malins was ploughing his field, near to what is now Huyton, when he noticed, out of the corner of his eye, a woman running through the woodland bordering the field. The farmer watched as the woman disappeared into the woods and observed that she had left a bundle of some sort at the base of a tree. He left his plough and went to investigate. It was a new-born baby girl swathed in rags. The farmer, a widower, decided to adopt her and called her Anna after his late wife.

Anna grew into a young woman of breathtaking beauty and every man she met was enchanted and infatuated with her. Anna could not understand her popularity and why, almost every day, some love-struck man proposed to her. There was no mirror in the farmhouse, so she was not aware of her beauty.

One chilly Christmas Eve afternoon in 1647, Anna, who had now turned twenty, left the farmhouse to gather wood, but never returned. Farmer Malins expressed his concern about Anna's safety to a neighbouring farmer and two woodsmen but they assured him that she was probably seeing a secret boyfriend and would soon return.

By midnight, there was still no sign of the girl, so Farmer Malins lit a torch and went into the woods. He found a piece of Anna's torn dress and picked it up. He shouted her name and scoured the woods and the countryside until the sun came up, but Anna was still nowhere to be found.

Three days later, the gossipers of rural Liverpool started malicious rumours that Jeremiah Malins had raped his adopted daughter and killed her after making her pregnant. These cruel whisperings spread like wildfire through the community and finally reached the ears of a Colonel Birch, a power-mad military commander stationed at the Tower of Liverpool. Birch and his soldiers visited Malins at his farm and accused him of rape and murder. Malins protested and was so outraged that he punched Birch in the face. To make matters worse, Birch found the piece of Anna's skirt on the table with buttons on it and an old woman came forward and said she had seen the farmer kissing and molesting the girl in the woods by the light of the moon on Christmas Eve.

Colonel Birch had heard enough and decided to force the farmer to confess. He chained him to the underside of a hay-cart which was then pulled by horses for two miles. At the end of the journey, Malins was unchained and Birch saw that the farmer's back had been badly scraped and was dripping with blood. Yet Malins still would not confess to killing Anna, so Birch transported him to the Tower of Liverpool in Water Street. There he was stripped naked and put on a rack where he was slowly stretched until his shoulder was pulled out of its socket and his ankle ligaments snapped. The farmer yelled out in agony, "Please have mercy!" But Birch was a renowned sadist and stood there drinking wine and sighing with pleasure. The farmer was removed from the rack and tied to a chair. His hands were bound to the arms of the chair and a masked man with a hammer entered the chamber. He put three-inch tacks under the Malins' finger nails and tapped them in slowly. When Malins screamed out for the man to stop, the torturer struck his kneecap with the hammer.

"You killed Anna, didn't you?" demanded the drunken Colonel Birch and gave the farmer an ultimatum. "Say you did and you'll be tortured no more."

"I didn't kill her, by almighty God, I swear I didn't," groaned Farmer Malins, blood trickling from his fingers.

The records of what happened next are unclear and unreliable but one version of events is that something unparalleled in the history of torture took place: Jeremiah Malins was squashed between two panels of wood which were nailed together, so that the farmer could hardly breathe. Then, the two chief carpenters of the Tower were ordered to saw down the length of the sandwiched panels with a long woodcutter's saw. When the blade was inches from the farmer's skull, he allegedly confessed to the murder but Colonel Birch ordered the carpenters to continue and despite the horrific screams, they sawed downwards through the farmer's head, slicing it in half. Birch told them to keep on sawing until they had cut through the body. A mob outside the Tower cheered when they heard the news of the execution and demanded to see the bisected body, which was later put on display.

Then, on New Years Day 1648, the missing girl returned, in the best of health, to the farmstead. The shocked community listened to her account of where she had been since that fateful Christmas Eve. Anna said that she had been travelling with a band of gypsy folk she had met in the woods. They had taken her to a fair in Chester on Christmas Eve and exhibited her in a sideshow as a direct descendant of Cleopatra.

When Anna was told that Farmer Malins had been tried for her murder and executed, she collapsed. Colonel Birch sent a messenger with an apology and then arrested old Mrs Todd, the woman who said she had seen the farmer molesting his daughter. Mrs Todd was taken to the Tower and a trainee executioner, a lad of fifteen, was allowed to hone his beheading skills on her. She was bundled to the chopping block, beside herself with fear. Two soldiers positioned her head over the chopping block and the young boy hit her neck squarely with the axe and her head flew across the room. As it fell to the chamber floor, it still seemed alive, the tongue squirming outside the mouth. Colonel Birch picked up the head and coldly exclaimed, "See how the gossiper's tongue still flaps, even in death!"

Resurrection Mary

In the autumn of 1995, a Wavertree couple moved into a beautiful old Victorian house near Druids Cross Gardens in the Calderstones area of south Liverpool. In the daytime, the house and garden seemed picturesque and quiet but when darkness fell, the atmosphere changed dramatically, and a series of supernatural occurrences sent the couple in search of a ghost researcher. They said that on most nights after ten o'clock, they heard the sound of something being dragged up the gravel path outside.

Whenever this sound was heard, the couple's dog Arthur would become hysterical and run upstairs in a terrible state. The couple's cat Jinjee, on the other hand, always went to the window and stared out into the darkness, as if she could see something. Jinjee was much braver than her owners because the couple never dared to look outside when they heard the eerie dragging sound. They just sat inside and held on to each other as they heard the 'thing' crawl up to the front doorstep and rap on the door for a while.

When the ghost researcher arrived, he taped the sounds and, on one occasion, he actually caught a glimpse of a hazy, white object on the gravel path and tried to photograph it. However, nothing appeared when the picture was developed. One night, when the dragging sound was heard, the ghost researcher went outside and saw pieces of gravel being dragged along with the invisible object. He researched the history of the house, determined to find out if anything unusual had happened there in the past. The ghostbuster passed the address to a circle of local historians and one of them found an interesting piece of information.

On the site, in 1750, Dr Charles Johnson had an affair with a young girl named Mary Jenkins. Mary was only eighteen but was exceptionally beautiful with long blonde hair, big blue eyes and pale, delicate skin. She was uneducated and worked as a maid for the doctor who, finding her irresistible, had an affair with her resulting in a pregnancy. Dr Johnson's wife died soon after the pregnancy became known and young Mary said that they could now be married and tell the world about their love. However, the doctor had other ideas and was set on marrying Georgina Clayton, who had recently inherited her father's fortune. Mary Jenkins pleaded with Dr Johnson, even getting down on her knees and saying, "Please say you will marry me. I'm having your child." Johnson would have none of it, he flew into a rage and hit her across the face. "Well then, I'll tell everyone about our love and our baby," sobbed Mary Infuriated, Johnson snatched a poker from the fireplace and struck his young lover on the head.

An old widow named Hannah Cleveland heard the screams and went to Johnson's cottage and peeped through the window. She saw him bending over Mary Jenkins, who looked lifeless, and the tearful doctor was saying, "Mary, my love … what have I done? Please open your eyes."

The Widow Cleveland scuttled off to the local vicar to tell him of the dreadful deed and he and a mob of locals turned up at the cottage, but there was no sign of young Mary. The poker was examined but had evidently been cleaned and had no blood on it. Doctor Johnson denied the attack had taken place and said he had not set eyes upon the maid for over two days. He said she often went missing and he believed her to be staying with a lover. Johnson claimed that Mrs Cleveland was mentally unbalanced and prone to hallucinations since the death of her husband, but the widow insisted that her story was true. The vicar said that, as there was no evidence of a murder, he could do nothing. But tongues in the community started wagging as the weeks passed and Mary Jenkins did not appear. Many believed that the Widow Cleveland had been telling the truth and that Johnson had disposed of Mary's body.

When Georgina Clayton, the woman Johnson was to marry, heard about Mary's strange disappearance, she asked him outright if he had killed her. Johnson became enraged and said, "I swear before almighty God! I only wish Mary Jenkins would return so she could prove my innocence! Believe me, I had nothing to do with her disappearance."

"I'm sorry I doubted you, Charles," said Georgina, accepting his innocence.

A week later, the couple married and enjoyed a short honeymoon in Scotland. When they returned, nobody would talk to them and the gossipers openly pointed at Johnson when he passed by in the street.

"They still maintain that you have something to do with Mary's disappearance," said Georgina, one stormy night at the cottage.

Johnson turned out all the lights and lit a candle. He took Georgina by the hand and led her up to the bedroom saying, "I've told you my dear, by the heavens above us, I wish Mary Jenkins would return to prove my innocence." At that precise moment, the couple heard a noise outside the cottage. Dr Johnson opened the window and there, down in the garden, was a horrible sight. In the moonlight, the half-decomposed body of Mary Jenkins was dragging itself along the path towards the house on its stomach. Johnson stared down at the ghoulish figure which returned his stare, reaching out a skeletal hand. The once beautiful eyes were set back in gaping black sockets and the once rosy cheeks had collapsed inwards. Suddenly the mouth opened and a faint voice cried, "Charles, I love you."

Johnson slammed the window shut and drew the curtains. Georgina asked him what he had witnessed because he was shaking like a leaf. His hand shook so badly that he had to put the candlestick down. He dashed to the bed and hid under the bedclothes like a frightened child.

"What's the matter, Charles?" Georgina cried, as she flung back the curtains and looked out of the window.

"No!" shouted the doctor from his bed. "Don't look out!"

But the seeds of doubt had been sown. She looked out and recoiled at the sight of the vile corpse, which had now dragged itself to the front step, its bony fingers clawing at the door. Georgina was suspicious about its identity and turned and scrutinised her new husband.

"That is Mary Jenkins, is it not?"

He begged her to come away but Georgina saw the guilt etched on his face and fled downstairs and escaped by the back door. Having told the vicar, he and a magistrate headed to Johnson's cottage with a mob hungry for justice. But they were cheated, because Johnson was found sitting up in bed, dead, with a look of terror on his face, his bulging eyes fixed on something. They followed his stare to the floor beside the bed, but there was nothing there, nor was there any corpse on the path outside. However, a search of the garden revealed the shallow grave of the badly decomposed body of Mary Jenkins and her unborn child.

For many years, the Johnson cottage remained empty, because people who lived there often reported hearing the sound of 'Resurrection Mary' dragging herself from her grave in the garden. The couple who recently moved into the house in Calderstones were none too pleased by the ghost researcher's chilling discovery ...

SURPRISE APPEARANCE
AT THE CAVERN

The following story concerns three men who used to visit the Cavern Club in Mathew Street, way back in the days before Merseybeat, when the Cavern was a jazz club. The story is told all over Liverpool and has been in circulation since the early 1960s. Nobody knows whether there is any truth behind the tale or if it is just a so-called 'urban myth'. Strangely enough, in every version of the story, the names of the characters are always the same. Furthermore, according to an article in the *Liverpool Echo* in the late 1950s, the manager of the Cavern claimed that there was a ghost that haunted the ladies' toilets ...

Around 1957, Alan Sytner opened the Cavern Club in Liverpool to provide a venue for the then thriving jazz scene. As most people know, the Cavern was basically a collection of arched warehouse cellars in the heart of downtown Liverpool where the Beatles first came to prominence.

In the late 1950s, three men went to the club one evening with their girlfriends and had a great time listening to the jazz bands. The men were Johnny, Tony and Peter and, at four in the morning, when most of the clubgoers had gone home, the three men and their girlfriends sat at a table, smoking and chatting away. The conversation turned from sport, to politics, to religion, to the meaning of life and finally resulted in an argument about the occult.

At this point, one of the men's girlfriends, a girl named Rita, said that one of the toilets in the Cavern was supposed to be haunted, but Peter, a hard-boiled sceptic, said it was probably just a publicity gimmick invented by the Cavern's owner. One of the managers overheard Peter's remark and insisted that there really was a ghost; one of the bouncers had recently seen it, it was a man dressed in black.

At this point, Johnny suggested that everyone present should gather round the table and join hands to summon the ghost, claiming that he knew the actual words to evoke a spirit. The girlfriends thought it would be exciting and urged their boyfriends and the bouncers to join in. Everyone thought it was a joke except a young man named Tony, who was not exactly religious but said the occult should not be treated in such a light-hearted manner. He sat at another table, lit up a cigarette and watched nervously. With everyone but Tony gathered round, Johnny said, "Right, turn off the lights and get a candle or something."

No candle could be found but someone brought a small electric torch and switched it on in the centre of the table. The lights were switched off and all the participants joined hands. Immediately there was a scream. One of the bouncers had put his hand up one of the girl's dresses for a laugh and Johnny said, "Stop messing about. We need absolute silence." There were a few sniggers but then a strange quiet descended in the cellar. After a minute, Johnny called out, "O Lord of darkness, I invite you into the Cavern. Give us a sign so we may believe."

One of the girls said, "And get a move on, 'cos I wanna go to the toilet."

A tall shadowy figure walked across the darkened room wearing a black suit and black polo-neck sweater, hardly in fashion at the time. His black fringe was slicked back in the style of the so-called 'DA cut' popularised by Tony Curtis. None of the girls was scared, the stranger was attractive, with magnetic eyes and they thought he was just a clubgoer who had been part of the stay-behind, but Tony, who was on his own at the other table, thought the man was evil from the moment he set eyes on him as he came out of the toilets.

"I am Lucifer," intoned the man, in a rich deep voice. Then smirked as he surveyed the shocked expressions of the people at the table.

"Stop messing about," said Johnny. "Can't you see we're trying to hold a seance here."

"You idiot," replied the stranger. "I am Lucifer. You didn't expect me to have horns, did you?"

"Oh, you're the Devil, like?" sneered one of the bouncers, trying to impress the girls.

"You'll notice that I haven't got hoofed feet either."

"Johnny, I'm scared. Turn the lights on," cried Rita.

"Relax, dear," said the stranger, "I'm not as bad as I'm painted."

"There's no such thing as the Devil," retorted Peter.

"If you believe in God, you must believe in me too," said the man in black, "… unless you're an atheist, of course."

"Yes I am, actually," said Peter in a matter-of-fact way.

"Then if you don't believe in me, can I have your soul?" asked the stranger.

Peter laughed nervously, "But I don't believe …"

"Give me your soul then!" shouted the stranger.

"Give him your soul, mate!" joked the bouncer and chuckled, "Soul – mate, gerrit?" But no one was laughing. The atmosphere had turned tense and frightening.

"Okay, take it then," said Peter, grinning uneasily.

"No! Don't, Peter! Don't!" shouted Tony from the other table. He stood up but was afraid to go over.

"Thank you," said the stranger reaching out in the direction of Peter with his hand and clutching at something in the air. The torch light began to fade until it was just a dim orange filament, then the Cavern was in complete blackness.

"That was one amateurish set-up," said one of the bouncers, almost falling over the table in the dark, as he went to switch on the lights … but they didn't work. "Oh, don't tell me the flippin' fuses have gone again," he said, groping about in the darkness.

A voice whispered in Tony's ear, "I'll be back for you one day and your god won't be able to save you."

"In the name of our saviour Jesus Christ I tell you to leave," said Tony, suddenly finding some courage from somewhere.

At that the lights came back on and everyone rose from the table – all but Peter, who slumped forwards, hitting his face on the table-top. He seemed to be drunk but when his mates got him back to his flat in Smithdown Lane, he didn't seem to be breathing. He was taken by a taxi to the Royal Hospital in Pembroke Place and was certified dead on arrival. The coroner who performed the post-mortem later said that Peter, who was twenty-seven, had the body of an eighteen year-old and seemed to have been in perfect health. A verdict of death by natural causes was recorded but all the people who attended the frightening seance believed that Peter had died because he had foolishly given permission to the Devil to wrench his soul from his body.

WHEN THE DEVIL
WALKED THROUGH LIVERPOOL

On 12 January 1866, a great snow storm struck Liverpool. The blizzard was so fierce that it blew down telegraph lines and all communication with London and the rest of the country was suspended for over a week. As temperatures plunged, the River Mersey froze over and Liverpool gradually came to a standstill, as people huddled indoors to escape the big freeze. Liverpool soon resembled a ghost town; not a soul roamed the snow-covered streets.

At six o'clock the following morning, a policeman in the south-end of the city came upon a curious sight. In the virgin snow on Great George Street, he noticed a trail of what seemed to be animal tracks. At first sight, the tracks looked like hoof prints but they were very peculiar. It was as if the animal had put one hoof exactly in front of the other and walked in a precise straight line. The policeman measured the distance between each horseshoe-shaped print and saw that it was eight inches. He knew of no animal capable of walking in such a manner.

He followed the trail and saw that nothing impeded the progress of the unidentified animal; the tracks going right up Great George Street and up either side of a factory wall. At one point, the tracks went across the roof of a snow-covered house in Oldham Street, where a postman had also noticed the strange prints. The trail extended up St Anne Street and Scotland Road where they suddenly came to a dead end, as if the strange creature had taken off like a bird.

News of the eerie trail spread across Liverpool and the local population, which included many superstitious Irish immigrants, thought there was something unearthly about the prints in the snow. People were soon referring to the tracks as the Devil's footprints, believing that Satan had strolled through the deserted streets of Liverpool, for who else had hoofed feet? they argued, and who else could walk over walls and rooftops? Some thought the culprit was Spring-Heeled Jack, whilst others blamed otters, rats, or even a three-legged horse. Perhaps the most outlandish theory was that the trail had been made by a rope dangling from a balloon! But none of the theories fitted the facts.

The mystery deepened when several people, including a postmaster in Richmond Row, Everton, claimed that they had heard strange pipe music at around four o'clock on the morning that the tracks were made. This convinced people that it was the Devil who has often been depicted as playing pipes like the Greek god of mischief, Pan.

After the thaw, the footprint incident soon faded from the public memory. However not many people in Liverpool knew that similar footprints had been seen eleven years earlier in Devon, in similar circumstances after a snowstorm. Also, in the reign of King Richard I, at York, a monk wrote about hoof-like tracks which appeared on the ground after a fierce lightning storm.

So, what made the tracks on that winter's morning in Liverpool? Was it just some wild animal like a badger that had ventured into a seemingly deserted town? Or did the Devil really once walk through Liverpool?

THE HOMESICK PASSENGER

In 1993, Alan, a Liverpool cab driver, bought a second-hand hackney cab from Brian, who lived in his street. The taxi seemed fine but when Alan was on night duty, it started acting very peculiarly. He was driving up Townsend Lane, near Cabbage Hall, to collect a woman in Cherry Lane, when the cab started slowing down. Suddenly, the steering wheel twisted itself left in the cabbie's hands and the cab turned down a street. Alan regained control of the vehicle and narrowly missed hitting a skip full of rubbish at the side of the road. He stopped and put on the handbrake. He turned the wheel to check the steering but it seemed okay and Alan started wondering if his tired mind was playing tricks on him. He put the incident down to an involuntary spasm in his left arm and drove on.

The place where the cab had stopped was Chapel Road and, at the end of the road, Alan turned the wheel right to turn into Manningham Road. However, on reaching a junction, the wheel again turned left of its own accord and this time Alan wrestled with the wheel to bring it back but the cab turned into Pinehurst Road, where he deliberately stalled it. He got on the phone to Brian, even though it was after midnight, and gave him a right earful although he insisted that there was nothing wrong with the steering. However, when Alan told him where the incident had happened, Brian fell silent, then said, "Did you say Pinehurst Road?"

"Yeah, that's right. Look, I'm coming round to your's now, if I can get there in this useless write-off that is."

Alan was a rather stocky man who didn't suffer fools

gladly and when he turned up at Brian's flat, he was very angry. Brian invited him in and tried to convince him that there was nothing wrong with the cab. After all, it had just had its MOT and was in pristine condition mechanically. He made Alan a strong coffee and calmed him down. Half an hour later, he was on the road again looking for fares and the remainder of that shift was trouble-free.

Over the next few weeks, Alan learned that the trouble with the steering only seemed to occur when the cab was in the vicinity of an area bounded by Townsend Lane, Utting Avenue and Priory Road. This obviously didn't make any sense but Alan's mate Eric, who was always reading books about UFOs, reckoned that there was a sort of mini-Bermuda Triangle around Anfield which might be affecting the mechanical workings of the cab.

Alan told him that his theory was ridiculous but, a month later, Alan picked up two young women outside the Grafton nightclub and dropped them off at their home in Arkles Lane, in Anfield. As he drove away, he glanced in his rear-view mirror and was startled to see a middle aged man with glasses on, sitting in the back of the cab. He stopped the cab and reached for a cosh that he carried under his seat for violent troublemakers.

As soon as Alan asked, "Where are you going mate?" the passenger bowed his head, as if he were going to sleep, and faded away into thousands of little flickering spots. Alan was more stunned than scared. He climbed into the back of his vehicle to inspect the space where he had just evidently seen a ghost, shook his head in confusion. A police patrol car turned up and one of the officers asked him what was wrong. When Alan said he had just seen a ghost, the policeman smirked at his colleague and then drove on.

A friend of Brian's later told Alan that a passenger had suffered a heart attack in the cab while the vehicle was travelling up Priory Road. Brian had watched the man slump forward and bow his head and then went to help him. He had realised that the man was seriously ill and called out, "Hang on, mate, I'll take you to Walton Hospital," but the man had spluttered, "No ... take me home ... I'd rather die there ... Take me home." Then clutched his chest and died.

Alan asked where the passenger's home had been. "I think it was either Pinehurst Road or Pinehurst Avenue," answered Brian's mate. Alan remembered that the cab's steering wheel had turned by itself into Pinehurst Road. It seemed as if the ghost had been trying to get the cab to drop its spirit off at home. He told Brian's mate about the incident. "I know," admitted Brian's friend, "that's why Brian sold the cab. It's haunted, but don't say I told you."

Alan later sold the haunted cab to another unsuspecting taxi driver, so it is still on the roads of Liverpool and, if recent accounts are to be believed, the vehicle is still carrying its ghostly home-sick passenger.

OVER THE WALL

In the 1970s, at a house off Liverpool's Myrtle Street, lived Sylvia, a woman in her early fifties. She was always leaning over the garden wall watching the comings and goings of her neighbours and consequently knew everyone's business. She had few friends except Peggy, who lived in nearby Myrtle Gardens, and who often stopped to chat to her but in 1980, Peggy moved to the Garston area of the city and lost touch with Sylvia.

One hot June evening in 1990, Peggy and her husband were driving to a friend's house near the Bluecoat School in the Wavertree area, when Peggy saw Sylvia leaning over a low stone wall near some bushes. Peggy said to her husband, "I don't believe it. It's Sylvia. Stop the car!"

Peggy's husband stopped and reversed the car until Sylvia came into view in his wing mirror. Peggy got out to talk to her old friend but Peggy's husband had never liked Sylvia and stayed in the car.

"How are you Sylvia?" Peggy asked, looking at her old friend, who had hardly changed.

"Alright. I came here in 1985. Don't like it up here though. It's very secluded," Sylvia replied, morosely.

Peggy noticed that her lips had a pale blue tinge and she asked her why.

"Oh, I think it's just my bad circulation," she replied, sounding very tired. It seemed like an enormous effort just for her to speak.

Peggy felt as if there was a barrier between them because they had not been in touch for so long. She asked her where she lived and Sylvia just nodded to a place on her side of the wall and said, "Over there."

"Church Road? What number? I'll call in sometime," said Peggy, rummaging in her handbag for a scrap of paper to write down the address. Sylvia just shook her head and said, "No it's okay; I don't want any visitors."

Peggy felt was taken aback by her rudeness, but still wrote her phone number down and handed it to Sylvia, saying, "Oh well, here's my number anyway; you can give me a call sometime if you want."

Sylvia didn't even take the piece of paper, so Peggy put it on the wall. Then Sylvia said, "I won't be calling you," and grinned.

This was too much, and Peggy started was thinking of an excuse to get back to the car, away from her antisocial friend, when Sylvia walked off without saying goodbye.

When Peggy got back in the car she told her husband about Sylvia's bad manners. "Don't know why you're so surprised," he said. "I never could stand that the woman."

Upon turning right at the top of the lane, Peggy and her husband suddenly noticed that there was a church on the corner and next to this church was a graveyard. So Sylvia had been leaning over the wall of this graveyard when talking to Peggy and this made the couple shiver.

Sometime later, they met the vicar of the church and learned that, in 1985, Sylvia had been buried near that wall at the exact spot where Peggy had chatted to her. Peggy nearly fainted when she realised she had been talking to a ghost. Sylvia had died from carbon monoxide poisoning from a faulty gas fire. That explained why she had blue lips.

MARRIED IN HASTE

The following incident has been investigated by writers and researches for over sixty years but no one has ever been able to explain it.

In 1930, twenty-five-year-old Cheshire woman, Eleanor May, was staying with her sister's family in Warwickshire in a little house situated on the periphery of Stratford-upon-Avon. One evening, Eleanor accompanied her sister Emily to a dance held in the local church hall. They danced all night and, by midnight, Emily had gone home to her husband, leaving her sister in the arms of a man who said his name was Freddie Barclay. He had receding blond hair, a distinguished aquiline nose, and was quite tall and handsome but he said very little, seeming rather shy. He said he was forty and that he worked for a local printer.

Eleanor was strongly attracted to Freddie and arranged to meet him at an old country pub called the Magpie and Crown at eight the following Thursday. The Magpie and Crown was a cosy pub with a thatched roof and a large blazing fire. It is rumoured that Shakespeare himself once drank at the tavern that once stood on the same site in the sixteenth century. After a pleasant evening, Freddie walked Eleanor home and promised to be at the pub the following week. He kissed her gently, then walked away.

Eleanor couldn't wait for the next Thursday. It eventually came and the couple were soon sitting in the corner, gazing at each other and holding hands. Freddie and Eleanor met regularly at this pub for about a month until, one evening, Freddie shocked her and all the drinkers in the pub, by going down on one knee and proposing. Eleanor was surprised but said she would love to marry him and they arranged to marry at the local Church of the Holy Trinity.

Emily was far more less enthusiastic about her sister's future husband and noticed things which made her suspicious. For one thing, he never talked about his home life, just saying that he lived with his domineering, old-fashioned mother; for another, he only ever mentioned the area where he lived, without actually specifying the address. She warned Eleanor to be wary of the printer but she seemed blinded by her love for him and said she trusted him implicitly.

"For all you know, he could have a wife and children tucked away somewhere. Bigamy is a very serious crime, you know," said Emily.

Eleanor was very upset by her reaction and accused her

of being jealous, because her own marriage was going through a rocky patch. Emily stormed off saying that she would certainly not be going to the wedding. Nevertheless, the wedding took place a month later and was a very simple affair indeed. Only Freddie, Eleanor, the barman from the Magpie and Crown and a few of the other drinkers were present. Freddie excused his mother's absence by saying she was too ill to attend.

After the ceremony, the barman and his regulars showered the newly-weds with rice and confetti and then there was a party back at the Magpie and Crown. It was there that events took a sinister turn. During the merrymaking and singing, Eleanor noticed that Freddie was absent. She asked the barman where he was and he said he had probably gone to the toilet, but Freddie was not there. In fact, Freddie was nowhere to be seen.

Days went by with no sign of him, yet Eleanor refused to take off her wedding dress. She told her sister what had happened but got no sympathy, "I told you there was something fishy about him and you attacked me. I've seen all these whirlwind romances before."

Humiliated, Eleanor then went to the village police station and reported her bridegroom's disappearance. The old sergeant seemed intrigued, "You'd better come through," he said, and escorted the young lady into his office, where he sat her down and offered her a drink.

"Look Miss ... ooh sorry ... missus. We've heard of this Freddie Barclay before. About ten years back ... he did the same thing then. Promised a young lady, just like yourself, that he'd marry her, then vanished."

"But I don't understand," sobbed Eleanor.

"Call me superstitious and let it go no further than these four walls, but I reckon this Mr Barclay is a ghost," whispered the sergeant, solemnly.

"A ghost?" said Eleanor, forlornly, taking the seat which the sergeant had offered her; her wedding gown now all crumpled and soiled around the hem.

The sergeant remained sombre-faced as he continued, "I took the liberty on the last occasion of checking up on Freddie Barclay. I discovered that a man of that name and description once worked at a printer's works, Maggs Brothers, about a mile away. He was about to marry a girl in the village who, by all accounts, looked very much like you but she left him at the altar. Freddie was inconsolable and took arsenic and died. His old widowed mother was devastated and she passed away herself soon afterwards from pneumonia, brought on by the shock."

"But my Freddie was no ghost ... He was real ... I kissed him," Eleanor told the old policeman, stifling back the sobs.

"That's exactly what the last girl told me. I can't say for certain that he was a ghost. But the last girl who was deserted by Freddie Barclay never saw him again. I showed her his grave in the cemetery outside of the Holy Trinity Church, where you were married."

Eleanor never could accept what the sergeant told her. She never married and never heard from the sinister Freddie Barclay. Several weeks after her husband's disappearance, Eleanor awoke to find her wedding ring was also missing. It was never seen again either.

Eaten Alive

The following grisly account is mentioned in some detail in a fascinating old book entitled *Days Gone By* by the Victorian folklorist GP Lucas.

In the centre of Liverpool, in the late eighteenth century, there stood a bakehouse in a narrow crowded street called Tempest Hey. The proprietor was an obese man named Andrew Pudsey who took great delight in torturing the many rats and mice that he caught in the cellars. Pudsey would sometimes take a large carving knife and slice the head off any unfortunate rodent he managed to catch. Often the rat's headless body would run around on the floor long after its decapitation. On other occasions, the sadistic baker would get a large skewer and impale a rat or mouse before barbecuing it slowly over an open fire.

On one occasion, he caught a poor skinny-looking mouse and ran a skewer through its hind-quarters whilst it was still alive. He then held it high over the flames of the blazing fire and said to a young apprentice, Raymond Smithy, "Listen, lad. Listen to its eyes popping." Raymond told Pudsey to stop but the cruel baker just grinned and listened with a look of delight as the poor animal squealed in agony.

One sultry evening in August 1792, the Tempest Hey bakehouse was busier than usual because of an order for 800 loaves for the Lord Mayor's banquet. Pudsey and young Raymond worked into the small hours to turn out all the bread, but Pudsey became fatigued by the effort and the unbearable heat and decided to have a catnap down in the cool cellar, telling Raymond to wake him in an hour's time. He drank a flagon of cold water, then took his lantern down into the cellar and lay on a pile of sacks containing flour. He stretched out and yawned and was soon asleep.

Some time later, Pudsey felt something heavy pressing down on his chest. He assumed it was Raymond waking him and said, "Alright, lad," but when the baker opened his eyes he saw a sight he hadn't bargained for. An enormous grey rat was on his chest, looking right into his eyes. Pudsey was so terrified, he just closed his eyes and prayed for the enormous rodent to get off him. A few seconds later, the rat hopped off and scuttled over to a dark corner, where there was a huge hole in the wall. This hole had been caused by subsidence and many of the bricks had crumbled away to leave a gaping opening about three feet in diameter. Pudsey had been meaning to brick it up but had not got round to it.

The baker took his lantern and was making his way up the stairs, when he noticed smoke coming from under the trapdoor leading to the bakehouse. He could hear the flames crackling and knew that he could not risk opening the door otherwise the flames would burst through. He panicked and decided that the only way out was through the hole in the cellar. He was scared of meeting the enormous red-eyed rat again, so he peeked into the hole and held the lantern out into the darkness. Several rats in the tunnel ran off in fright and Mr Pudsey started inching his way through the opening but, because he was so fat, his enormous gut became lodged in the hole. He was jammed tight, unable to move forwards or back and he started to curse.

Up in the bakehouse, Raymond was lying on the floor, overcome with smoke from the blaze, which had been caused by the overheated oven. A nightwatchman from the building next door broke in and rescued the apprentice but Pudsey was not so lucky. The roof of the cellar began to cave in and flaming chunks of wood and mortar showered the sacks of flour. Several of the rats hiding in nooks and crevices in the cellar fled towards the large hole which they used as an exit and entrance but Pudsey's was blocking the way. The rats started to nibble and gnaw frantically at his obese body in a desperate effort to escape the flames. The baker's futile screams only served to spur them on. One large rat even gnawed and scraped its way into the baker's buttocks and actually burrowed into the lower intestines of his body. He must have suffered an unimaginably agonising death.

The fire was extinguished an hour later and the body of Andrew Pudsey was recovered. The dead man's face was contorted with anguish and seeing it, Raymond the apprentice began to cry. The old nightwatchman pointed to a jagged gaping hole in the corpse's backside where blood was oozing out. The tip of a rat's tail was visibly dangling out of the hole. Everyone shuddered when a bloodsoaked half-dead rat fall out of the deep gaping wound, having gorged itself on the baker's flesh.

The gruesome tale of the sadistic baker does not end there. In 1801, grave diggers in Mulberry Street cemetery had to run for their lives one morning when they unearthed a nest of rats while digging a grave. The rats had been feeding on corpses and had burrowed a labyrinth of tunnels under the ground. When a ratcatcher smoked out the rodents, the full extent of the damage inflicted by the hungry underground desecraters was revealed. The contents of one coffin had been particularly ravaged. This was the coffin of Andrew George Pudsey. Even in death he was still providing fodder for the rats he had once delighted in torturing.

Lightning Persecution

There is an old but incorrect saying that, 'lightning never strikes in the same place twice'. In fact, there are many rangers in America's Yellowstone Park who have been struck more than three times while patrolling the park's wide open spaces and some have been killed by the searing bolts of electricity. Closer to home, in North Wales, there was one unfortunate man who was actually victimised by lightning in the middle of the nineteenth century.

One morning in 1857, Horace Pym, the twenty-year-old son of Sir Walter Pym, a wealthy landowner and ruthless businessman, left his family's sprawling mansion on the outskirts of St Asaph. He rode on horseback around the Welsh countryside, until he spotted Megan, a beautiful Welsh girl, who was standing on a hill, throwing corn to the birds. Horace Pym rode up to Meg and dismounted. He told her that he was the son of Sir Walter Pym but she could barely understand English. Horace took her lack of comprehension for rudeness, and raised his hand to her. Megan flinched but Horace did not actually hit her, but he did relish the way the girl looked so afraid of him. She called out something in Welsh, upon which a large bird of prey swooped down and attacked Horace, causing him to fall to the ground and roll down the hill. The girl then shouted out some more words in her native tongue, which frightened Pym's horse and sent him bolting out of the area. Horace Pym could not believe the situation he had found himself in and vented his fury on the girl. Some accounts say that he also raped her.

As Pym turned away, Meg started crying and pointing to the skies shouting something that Pym could not understand. As he ran off, the clouds overhead darkened ominously and soon it was bucketing down with rain. Thunder rumbled through the hills and a bolt of forked lightning struck Pym. The bolt pierced his scalp and burnt holes in his feet. He fell to the ground, unconscious.

When he awoke night had fallen and he felt seriously ill. Somehow he managed to stumble his way home, before collapsing at his father's feet. When he had been revived by the family physician, he muttered that he had been attacked by Welsh peasants who had tried to rob him. Pym's father was outraged and sent a posse of men armed with shotguns to the area but all they found was young Megan and her mother, who lived in a run-down cottage. One of Pym's men knew that Megan and her mother were regarded as witches and advised that they be left alone. Megan's mother Sian was known throughout the valleys as a horse-whisperer; someone who could communicate with all beasts of burden. She had evidently taught her magical gift to her daughter, who had been seen talking to foxes and birds.

The men returned to their master's estate and told Sir Walter that there were no peasants in the area where young Horace said he had been attacked. Sir Walter shared his son's violent streak and hit him with a riding whip and ordered him to stay in his quarters for a week.

A few days later, a terrible thunderstorm descended on St Asaph and ravaged Sir Walter's estate. Several of his men were killed by the lightning and during the fearful storm, young Horace hid under his bed, terrified of being struck by lightning once again. When the storm seemed to have abated, Horace crept over to the window and peeped out at the retreating clouds. As he did so, a powerful flash of sheet lightning zapped his face, temporarily blinding him. The surge of electrical energy was of such ferocity, that it actually scorched an image of Horace's face on to the window pane. This 'lightning picture', as it became known, remained etched on the window until the mansion was demolished in 1900.

After he had recovered, Horace was sent to Preston to supervise his father's printing business and died a year later after falling from his horse in 1860. A week after his burial, a thunderstorm raged over Preston and a bolt of lightning shattered Horace Pym's gravestone.

The Finger of Suspicion

In 1812, Duncan McPhail, a poor baker from the Everton district of Liverpool, was facing financial hardship. A local rival was selling his bread more cheaply and had a team of hard-working delivery boys to boot. The rival baker was rapidly driving McPhail out of business, so the latter decided to resort to a life of crime. He began by visiting a graveyard in Mulberry Street, Edge Hill, in the dead of night, equipped with a spade and lantern. He dug into the grave of a local doctor who was rumoured to have been buried with his jewellery. McPhail took an hour to smash through the coffin lid but saw to his delight that the doctor's hands had gold rings on almost every finger and in the silk-lined coffin there was a silver snuff box, a solid gold pendant and a gold watch and chain. McPhail prised off the rings, then snatched all the doctor's personal treasures. The first rays of the sun were appearing on the eastern horizon, so McPhail clambered out of the hole without even bothering to disguise his dirty work.

A week later, McPhail returned to the graveyard on a similar mission, but was almost caught by a nightwatchman who had seen his lantern among the gravestones. McPhail decided that grave-robbery was too dangerous and physically demanding, so he resorted to Plan B – robbery with violence. Dressed in black, with a silk scarf covering the lower half of his face, McPhail secreted himself in dark alleyways in the town after midnight, hoping to pounce on any vulnerable drunk who looked affluent enough to be worth coshing.

He found such a victim when Samuel Jones, a cotton merchant, came staggering out of a tavern which stood in a street that is now Pembroke Place. McPhail crept up behind the drunken merchant and delivered a succession of hefty blows with a weighted stick to the back of the man's head. Blood showered the robber during the frenzied attack and his scarf fell off. After dragging his victim into the alleyway, McPhail emptied his pockets of money and ripped off his watch and chain. Only then did he notice that Jones's eyes were wide open and lifeless. He was now a murderer! Suddenly, the voice of an old woman cried out in the darkness, "You've killed him!" McPhail panicked and searched the alleyway, determined to silence his only witness, but when he failed to find her, he ran home, keeping to the shadows.

The following morning, two detectives and a soldier arrested McPhail on a charge of murdering Samuel Jones and they presented their witness: the old woman who had seen the brutal killing. The sinister-old crone, whose face was almost covered by a black funeral shawl, pointed an accusing finger and said, "His shoes and arms were covered in blood."

McPhail laughed derisively and pointed to his shoes and arms, from which he had thoroughly scrubbed every last trace of blood. He had also hidden the money he had taken from Jones. The detectives were about to admit defeat and let the baker go, when the old woman said she was a gypsy and knew how to identify a murderer. If she were to utter an ancient spell, the corpse would point to the person who had taken its life. With no other witnesses or clues, the detectives agreed to the woman's proposition and ordered McPhail to the mortuary where the lifeless body of Samuel Jones was lying on a slab. Already, McPhail was twitching with nerves as he kept protesting his innocence.

The woman began reciting three phrases in an unknown language, then in a loud voice said, "Samuel Jones, here you lie, point to the one who caused you to die."

After about five seconds, the corpse's livid white arm began to twitch, then slowly rose from under the sheet and its pale index finger pointed directly at McPhail. The murderer moved about nervously, but wherever he went, the finger followed. He gave a little feigned laugh and said, "I know how it's done. Someone's under the sheet playing on my wits." He then grabbed the sheet, thinking to expose the detectives and fake gypsy as idiots for trying to stage such a charade. As he pulled the sheet away the ravaged body of Samuel Jones was revealed. The hair was matted with dried blood; the face bruised black and blue. The eyes were still open but the eyeballs were white.

As McPhail screamed out at the sight of his handiwork, the arm dropped. He tried to run out of the room but was apprehended by the detectives and made to confess all the deplorable crimes he had committed, including the murder of Samuel Jones. The baker signed his statement which proved to be his own death warrant, because a month later, he was hanged on the gallows at Kirkdale.

Having brought McPhail to justice, the old gypsy woman mysteriously disappeared and was never seen again.

THE REAL JEKYLL AND HYDE

Most people have heard or read of Robert Louis Stevenson's disturbing tale of dual personality, *The Strange Case of Dr Jekyll and Mr Hyde*, first published in 1886. Some think that Stevenson based his story on the double life of Edinburgh's Deacon Brodie, who was a respectable businessman by day and a vicious thief by night. But there was also a real-life Jekyll and Hyde character at large in Liverpool in the mid-nineteenth century.

Richard Rawlins was a fairly wealthy engineer who had shares in several Cornish tin mines as well as the Liverpool to Manchester Railway. He was said to be a tall, dark, handsome man with a fine voice and a rather shrewd nature. He had married three times, each marriage ending after a year because of Rawlins' dramatic mood swings and strange dual personality.

From childhood onwards, Rawlins claimed he had a naughty 'twin' inside him called Ralph. The young child even changed hands to write and draw when Richard became Ralph. Ralph had a nasty, mischievous personality and delighted in pulling the legs off spiders, whilst Richard was a nice friendly lad who picked flowers for his mother. It was Richard's mother who had innocently christened Richard's 'twin', after her son had told her about the imaginary double who lived inside him. Richard called his alter ego "the other fellow", but Mrs Rawlins suggested the name Ralph, which had been her grandfather's name.

A children's doctor was baffled at the child's split personality disorder and surmised it was just young Richard's way of getting attention. However, during adolescence, Richard became Ralph more often, usually when he had undergone an emotional time, or had been involved in any kind of accident. When sixteen year-old Richard broke up with his girlfriend Lottie, he broke down in tears in Toxteth Park. A policeman approached and asked him what was the matter, upon which the rejected Romeo's angelic face suddenly became twisted and his eyes squinted at the police officer. Richard had become Ralph and he spat in the policeman's face and ran out of the park shouting abuse at passers-by. Upon reaching his home in Duke Street, the mentally unstable teenager was attacked by his dog Samson, a huge black Labrador. The dog loved Richard but always growled and shied away from Ralph.

The teenager hurled himself into the front parlour and suffered a fit. He was found by the maid, biting into the hearth rug and foaming at the mouth. As she called for Richard's father, the boy passed out. When he was revived with smelling salts, he told his bewildered parents that Ralph had spat at a policeman and screamed abuse at people in the street on his way home.

The weeks went by without any reappearance of Ralph and Richard seemed happy and normal enough. Only occasionally did he swap his pen to his left hand and even then there were only minor variations in his handwriting style and behaviour. As the weeks and months turned into years, it looked as if the rebellious Ralph had thankfully disappeared forever into the depths of Richard Rawlins' subconscious. But in 1845, a dramatic accident brought Ralph back into Richard's life with a vengeance.

Richard Rawlins was now a twenty-five-year-old mining engineer who had already patented several explosive devices for blasting quarries and mines. On 1 November

1845, he entered the Dale Street premises of Rodney Hart, a gunsmith and gunpowder supplier, intending to purchase five pounds of gunpowder to test out a detonation device he was working on for the mines. Whilst he was there, a young apprentice in the shop's cellar carelessly dropped a flintlock he had just loaded and the gun went off, blasting a hole in a barrel of gunpowder. The apprentice was killed instantly and only certain parts of his dismembered body were later found. The shop-owner Rodney Hart was blown through the windows of the premises but survived.

Richard Rawlins was blown up on to the first floor of the devastated shop by the tremendous force of the blast. He was found hanging over a beam, barely alive, and suffering from concussion. He was treated at his Duke Street home by several distinguished physicians from a Rodney Street surgery and, for a week, it looked as if the young man would remain in a persistent comatose state. Amazingly, he pulled through or – at least – Ralph pulled through, as Richard's personality had evidently been destroyed in the explosion.

As soon as the young man was able to get out of his bed, he practically raped his maid and then assaulted the cook who was a sixty year-old woman. He stole over one hundred guineas from his father's room and then escaped by climbing dangerously out of a garret window. He scampered across the rooftops and then went on a crime spree, committing two burglaries in the Islington district, sexually assaulting three young women in Everton and almost battering a pub landlord to death because the ale he served was slightly sour. Unlike the meek Richard, Ralph had the strength of a wild animal and seemed to take delight in pitting his wits against the police. The wayward Ralph Rawlins was finally cornered in Vauxhall Road a week later by eight policemen armed with batons. The troubled young man had just set fire to a soap warehouse, causing damage estimated to be about one thousand pounds. Sadly, a single blow to the skull from a policeman's riot baton, instantly did what the explosion had failed to do. The man with two personalities suffered a massive brain haemorrhage and died with blood gushing from his nose and ears.

After his death, surgeons at the Liverpool Medical Institute in Mount Pleasant were eager to get to the bottom of the dead man's double personality and sought permission to open up his skull. At first Ralph's father refused permission, but later had a change of heart, as he too was curious to learn the reason for his son's illness.

A surgeon sawed open the skull and was flabbergasted by what he found: there were two brains tightly pressed together in the skull case, or four hemispherical lobes in all. The surgeon concluded that Richard was meant to have been one half of a twin when he was conceived. The other twin failed to develop into an embryo but retained its brain, which grew alongside the brain of its twin.

Undoubtedly, one of the brains contained the personality of Richard and the other the spiteful counterpart which asserted itself as Ralph. The Rawlins family naturally did not want society to know the details of their freakish son, so the findings of the Medical Institute were filed away for posterity.

KING OF THE DOCK ROAD

The following true story must rank as one of the blackest comedies in the history of Liverpool.

In the year 1870, there was a disreputable public house situated on the waterfront near Mann Island called the Black Horse, where the shady villains of Liverpool's underworld used to congregate. According to legend, the landlord of this squalid watering hole was a direct descendant of Dick Turpin, the famous highwayman. This legend was once thought to be nonsense but it is now known that Turpin actually visited Liverpool with his fellow rogue Tom King, in the early 1730s, whilst on the run.

The landlord was Joe Tyler and he called himself 'King of the Dock Road'. Any thieves or burglars caught operating on his manor were brought before him and faced two options: either they joined his establishment and gave him half of their loot, or they were turned over to the police.

One day, in January 1870, an unfortunate burglar from outside the area made the mistake of breaking into the Black Horse at four in the morning. Joe Tyler came charging downstairs after hearing a tinkle of glass breaking and caught the burglar, John Peters, aged just thirteen. Peters was halfway through the window when Tyler grabbed hold of him. He called for his wife Lizzie, who came running down in her nightgown and between them they held the youth with a revolver to his head. When she saw how young the burglar was, she took pity on him and said, "Give him a good hiding, then let him go home with a sore backside. Here, I'll give the cheeky beggar a good spanking myself!"

"Get away, woman!" said Joe angrily, Dragging the boy by his hair to the cellar. Joe told his wife to get some rope and something to gag with which to gag him.

The boy was held at gunpoint amongst the barrels of beer while Lizzie bound him up with rope.

"Tie him up tighter than that! Don't mollycoddle him!" Joe ordered his wife.

"Ah, but he's just a child, and a nice looking one at that," said Lizzie sympathetically.

"Never pity a thief, Lizzie. They'll rob your eyes and spit in the sockets if you feel sorry for them. He was trying to rob the place … remember," said Joe.

Lizzie thought about her husband's words then tightened the rope, saying, "Yeah! You little blighter!"

"What's your name?" Joe asked the little criminal.

"John Smith," replied the kid, nervously.

Joe Tyler pointed the revolver between his eyes, "Never lie to Joe Tyler! I'm the King of the Dock Road, and no one lies to me."

"Yeah, no one lies to Joe, not even me," said Lizzie, adding, "his great grandfather was Dick Turpin, y'know."

"So tell me who you are, or I'll shoot you and they'll be finding your bones in this cellar in a hundred years' time," said Joe.

"John Peters," whimpered the little burglar, about to cry.

"Good, now we're getting somewhere," said Joe, smiling. "Now, lad, why did you try to break into my place?"

The boy shrugged.

"Don't shrug at me or I'll break your collar bone. Someone put you up to it didn't they?"

"No sir," sobbed the boy.

Joe Tyler was paranoid and was always convinced that crooks from other areas of the city were trying to move on to his patch. He was convinced that the boy had been sent to break into the pub to make him look like an incompetent fool, so he slapped the boy's face and growled, "Who sent you?"

The boy blurted out, "I don't know his name but he had a beard and moustache and a mole on his face."

"That's more like it, boy!" said Joe, strutting up and down the cellar, racking his brains trying to think of somebody who fitted that description. Suddenly, there was a heavy knocking at the pub door and a voice shouted, "Police! Open up!"

Joe Tyler's legs turned to jelly. He had stolen property stacked in every nook and cranny of the upstairs rooms, so he quickly hid the revolver and told his wife to gag the child while he answered the door. "Hello constables," said Joe innocently. As they were asking if everything was alright, a loud scream was heard from the cellar. The little burglar had deliberately brought his bound feet down heavily on Lizzie's foot. The policemen ordered Tyler to open the door and when they went downstairs, they saw the boy tied up. Tyler explained what had happened and the police took the boy away, warning Tyler not to take the law into his own hands next time.

The following night, Joe Tyler and his mob waited until an old caretaker named Bob Woods came into the pub. He had a beard and moustache and a mole on his face, so they reckoned he had to be the instigator of the break in. When Woods walked in and asked for a beer, Joe Tyler gave the nod and two of his men threw a sack over his head and bundled him down to the cellar. Most of the clientele were criminals and they all crowded into the cellar, excitedly waiting for the kangaroo court to begin.

Joe Tyler sat on his specially made, high-backed chair to preside over the makeshift court, as Woods was cross-questioned about his attempts to turn Tyler and his men into laughing stocks. Woods ended up crying and pleading to go home but Tyler decided to play his old trick of ordering the accused to be executed by a tall muscular man wearing a black hood with two eye-holes. Woods was blindfolded and made to bend over with his head on a chopping block. The 'executioner' lifted a wet mop over Woods, whilst Joe said solemnly, "Bob Woods, you have been found guilty of trying to undermine the prestige of Joe Tyler and his associates and of instigating burglary so, as you refuse to admit your guilt, I hereby sentence you to have your head chopped off. Go ahead, executioner!"

The crowd of crooks looking on pretended to cry out in horror as poor Bob Woods trembled. The executioner grinned and handed the mop to Joe Tyler, who slapped its wet head down hard against the nape of Woods' neck. Everyone laughed but Bob lay there like a rag doll. Unbeknown to Tyler and his crew, he had a weak heart and had died from shock. This lethal sick joke proved to be a turning point and Tyler's cronies soon deserted him and two of them who secretly hated him informed the police. Meanwhile, John Peters confessed that he had made up his story about a bearded man because he thought Tyler was going to kill him if he stayed silent.

Tyler went on the run for two days while police searched the area. He hid in a dock warehouse, then boarded a ship *City of Boston* at Liverpool Docks under an assumed name. The ship sailed for New York where the self-styled 'King of the Dock Road' probably dreamt of setting himself up in criminal underworld, but history records that the ship Tyler boarded was lost at sea.

Night Terror

If this story doesn't keep you awake at nights, then nothing will. At a house in Moreton, in July 1863, Stewart Parker, a retired hangman, was sitting up in bed next to his wife reading a book, when he fell asleep. The time was just after one o'clock in the morning. An hour later, Mrs Parker woke up and turned over to see her husband fighting for his breath. He was drenched in sweat and making awful choking noises. She called his name repeatedly but he would not wake up. Mrs Parker knew that her husband had a weak heart and was fearful lest the nightmare he was having would kill him. She slapped him across the face but to no avail. As a last resort, she poured a glass of water over his face and shook him violently. His eyes flew open but he seemed to be paralysed for a few moments. Then he grabbed at his throat and in a raspy dry voice said, "Thank God! ... It was just a dream."

Mrs Parker told him she thought he was gone for a moment and asked him what he was dreaming about.

"I dreamt that a man in a black hood came towards me. He said his name was Peter Woods."

"Who is he?" asked Mrs Parker.

Her husband looked worried, "An old housebreaker who was hanged for the murder of a widow in Ashton town. After he was hanged, the real murderer was caught and confessed. Peter Woods said he'd return to haunt me, the jury and the judge. He said he had gypsy blood in him."

"Oh, it was just a nightmare," said Mrs Parker. "Take no notice." She shook her head when noticed saw the wet patch she had caused with the glass of water.

"But it was a horrible dream, dear," replied her husband

and told her the rest of it. "Woods tied my hands behind me and put a strap round my ankles, then pushed me so I was standing on the trapdoors of a gallows. Just as he put the noose over my head, you woke me up. I'm not that keen to go back to sleep now."

"Oh don't be so silly. You ate toasted cheese before you went to bed, didn't you?" said Mrs Parker.

"Yes, I know what you think, but I've never had a nightmare so real before," replied Mr Parker.

"Cheese can do that," said his wife. "It's well known that cheese upsets the brain when you sleep."

Half an hour later, Mr Parker fell asleep and, at around half past three, his wife woke to hear an unusual snoring sound. It was her husband having another dream. This time she had to push him out of bed and roll him across the floor to wake him. He staggered to his feet, gasping for air and threw the window open so he could inhale the fresh air.

"Are you alright? Shall I call a doctor?"

"No. It was Woods again," gasped Mr Parker. "He tried to hang me again. This time the trapdoor opened. I fell through and was hanging but you woke me in time. Am I going insane?"

By twenty to five the couple were drowsy and were already laughing at the ordeal and now Mr Parker really did seem ready for a good night's sleep. He kissed his wife, rolled over and went straight to sleep. The next morning at eight o'clock, his wife woke up to find him dead. His face was purple, the veins bulging. His eyes were open and protruding out of their sockets. Mrs Parker ran to her sister in the next street and a doctor was summoned. After examining Mr Parker he stated that he had died of a heart attack brought on by what is known as a 'night terror', a traumatic and extremely lucid nightmare, in which the dreamer is unable to wake up. Night terrors are rare, but there are around ten cases reported in England each year.

The pathologist was at a loss to explain a reddish band around Mr Parker's neck, such as was often found on the neck of a hanged criminal, caused by rope-burn from the noose. The coroner surmised that it was produced by haemorrhaging of the blood vessels in the neck caused by the coronary, but when Mrs Parker saw the strange mark on her deceased husband's neck, she immediately knew that Peter Woods had somehow exacted his revenge.

BREAK-IN AT THE GHOST HOUSE

The following strange incident was investigated by the old West Lancashire police force, back in the days before the Merseyside force was formed.

It was Autumn, 1966 and a dense blanket of thick fog had rolled across the Northwest, causing many fatal car accidents. The fog did not lift for three whole days, and one night during this murky period, two petty burglars, Richard and Carl, were prowling around Maghull, on the northern outskirts of Liverpool, taking advantage of the camouflaging fog. They tiptoed to a cottage near the village of Lunt, but an Alsatian dog chased after them when the flu-stricken Richard sneezed, so they decided to scout around in another area. They finally located the type of place they were looking for at half past two in the morning, on the outskirts of Ince Blundell. It was a magnificent Elizabethan-style mansion and it stood in the middle of a secluded field near the bottom of a hill. They sneaked up the path to the huge oak door where Richard read the plate, which said 'Magpie House' in delicate gold letters. He took out a hanky and blew his nose; his flu was getting worse and the cold foggy night was not helping.

Carl peeped through the windows and said, "Cor, look at the gear in there, Richie. It's like an Aladdin's Cave."

"It's probably alarmed. Be careful," warned Richard taking out a roll of sticky tape and looked about. After tearing off six strips and sticking them across the window, he wrapped a piece of cloth around the crowbar he carried and tapped the window gently until the pane cracked and fragmented. Richard gently peeled away the strips of tape with the pieces of window pane were stuck to them and Carl reached in through the hole and grabbed the handle, pulling the window wide open. Both men waited tensely, expecting an alarm to go off at any minute, but there was just silence.

The burglars climbed into the house and located two silver candlesticks with candles in them on the marble mantelpiece. Richard took out his lighter and lit them, then each thief took one and surveyed what seemed to be the parlour. A huge framed oil painting of a rural country scene in the style of Constable hung over the fireplace, but it was too bulky to carry out of the house. Richard and Carl then sneaked upstairs to another room, passing a spooky suit of armour on the landing. In this room was a grand piano and several smaller oil paintings. Richard stowed them under his arm while Carl ransacked a cabinet in the corner. It contained no money, so the thieves continued on their robbing expedition. In another room, Carl grabbed another pair of solid silver candlesticks and Richard nabbed himself a small ornamental gold clock.

Suddenly, a strange noise sounded in the house which stopped the thieves in their tracks. "What was that?" whispered Carl, his eyes darting about anxiously.

"Ssshhh!" hissed Richard, listening intensely. "Sounds

like someone snoring upstairs. Let's go and take a look."

"No way, let's get out of here. We've got a decent haul," said Carl, who had got a fit of the jitters.

"Pull yourself together," Richard snapped, under his breath. "Look, the toffs usually have all their jewellery and stuff in their bedrooms. So let's go and have a look. Don't start turning yellow on me now."

"Aw, come on, Richie, don't be greedy. We've got enough," complained Carl.

But Richard grabbed his friend by the arm and pulled him towards the bedrooms.

The snoring was getting louder and Richard grinned as he slowly turned the handle of the bedroom door. Ever so gently, he inched the door open to reveal an old man lying in bed, snoring like a train. The man looked very old-fashioned and quaint with his pointed nightcap with a bobble at the end and his huge droopy walrus moustache. The bed was an old four-poster, but what alarmed the burglars was that the old man was cradling an old-fashioned blunderbuss gun with a ridiculous cone shaped barrel. On seeing the gun, Carl said, "That's it, Richie! I'm quitting right now, pronto."

"Wait a minute, you yellow belly. Look!" whispered Richard pointing to a rusty metal box under the four-poster bed. "That's got to be his savings or something. We can't quit now. We're that close. That old geezer's probably too deaf to hear Gabriel's Horn." Richard's avarice had got the better of him and with the clock tucked under his arm, he sneaked across the room towards the bed, one agonising step at a time, each step seeming like an eternity. Carl remained rooted to the spot in the doorway, clutching the stolen candlesticks and several small paintings.

Richard knelt down by the bed and carefully dragged out the metal box. Putting the clock down he prised off the lid to reveal every burglar's dream: a hoard of gold coins mixed up with silver and gold rings. Suddenly, the clock Richard had taken from downstairs started to chime three o'clock. It was a moment of sheer terror. On the first chime, Richard ducked under the bed, and the man mumbled something in his sleep. On the second chime the old man put his finger on the trigger of the blunderbuss and upon the final chime he shouted out, "Damn clock! Be quiet."

He started snoring again, so Richard slid out from under the bed with sweat trickling in his eyes and picked up the metal box. He stood up and looked at Carl, who, like him, was sweating profusely. As Richard was tiptoed across the room, he suddenly stopped and closed his eyes. His nose twitched and he opened his mouth, about to sneeze.

"Noooo!" said Carl, under his breath, anticipating the noise his friend was about to produce.

"Aaaaashhooooo!!!" Richard could no longer suppress the sneeze, which echoed around the bedchamber. The old man shot up like a jack-in-the-box, saw the intruders, took aim with his blunderbuss and blasted Richard in the buttocks. He dropped the metal box causing the coins and countless rings to scatter everywhere. The burglars flew down the stairs, jettisoning their booty as they ran. They leapt out of the open ground-floor window into the foggy night and ran until they had no breath left in their bodies.

Richard went to hospital to have the buckshot removed from his behind and a suspicious doctor alerted the police. Detectives turned up and began questioning Richard. A detective warned that he would not get the buckshot removed until he told them exactly what he had been involved in. The burglar was nearly passing out with the pain, so he confessed to the attempted housebreaking. However, when the police went to the spot where Magpie House had stood, they found nothing but old ruins. A local farmer told them that old ruins were all that remained of Magpie House, which had been demolished in 1910. It seemed that the burglars had broken into a phantom house and, understandably, the police discontinued their investigation.

OLD BOB

The following incident took place in Liverpool in 1988 and was witnessed by four people, including a policewoman.

In November 1987, fifty-two-year-old Irene, suffered a minor stroke which left her partially paralysed down her left side, which meant that she had difficulty walking. Her fourteen-year-old daughter Carla looked after her outside school hours but Irene was too proud to have a home help, so she hobbled about the house with a walking stick.

In the summer of 1988, an opportunity arose for Carla to go to France with her school, but she was worried that her mother would be unable to cope without her. Irene insisted that her daughter should go on the trip, telling her that the effects of the stroke were wearing off and that she was improving each day. That night, Carla burst into tears and hugged her mum saying, "I'll stay with you, Mum. It wouldn't feel right having a good time in France while you're suffering here."

"Don't be silly, Carla," said Irene, firmly. "You're going to France. You deserve a break after looking after me all the time. Is that a deal?"

Carla sniffled and nodded. By the following week she was having fun in the South of France with her schoolfriends.

Despite her insistence on Carla going, Irene felt insecure in the house on her own and looked forward to Carla's phonecall from France to tell her she was well. One morning at three o'clock, Irene woke to hear a rattling noise coming from downstairs. She initially thought it was Carla returning from holiday but when she got out of bed and limped to the window, she froze. Two tall men in black ski hats were attempting to break in. One was standing at the gate in the front of the house keeping watch, while his colleague was forcing the door open with a small crow bar.

Irene's heart began to pound with terror; she must phone the police, but as there was no phone in her bedroom, she would have to get downstairs into the hall before the thugs broke in. As she opened her bedroom door, she heard a splintering sound, then heard the front door fly open and a stranger's deep voice saying "Hurry up!"

Irene almost fainted with fear as the burglars came into the house. She shouted out to an imaginary husband, "John! There's someone downstairs!" but the burglars laughed and took no notice. They had been keeping a watch on the house and knew that Irene was a practically housebound invalid with no husband. The sound of heavy footsteps pounded on the stairs and one of the tall burglars shouted, "You stupid cow! Come here!"

Irene staggered back into her bedroom, closed the door behind her and leaned against it, whispering, "Please God, don't let him in!" Suddenly, there was a loud grunting noise as the burglar fell down the stairs. Similar noises followed and then the sound of a dog barking. A blue flash of light lit up the bedroom as a police patrol car and police van arrived at the scene. Irene looked out of the window and watched the two burglars run straight into the arms of the policemen outside. Once the men had been apprehended, one of the policemen entered the house to reassure Irene, telling her a neighbour had phoned them after seeing the burglars trying to break into her home. He then added, "I think your dog's done a runner, love."

Irene looked puzzled.

"Your dog. There's no sign of it. But don't worry, it'll come back," the policeman continued.

"I haven't got a dog, officer," said Irene and recalled the strange growling noises she had heard when the burglars entered the house.

"Well one of the rogues down there has got a fair-sized bite on his backside. He said your Alsatian went for him."

"But I swear, officer, I haven't got a dog," said Irene. "The last Alsatian I had died years ago."

"It's okay," the policeman said, "we won't prosecute you or anything. I'm made up that fella got bitten. We've been after him for months."

Irene still insisted she did not own a dog and the policeman called in a policewoman to make a cup of tea for her as she was still trembling.

About half an hour later, when the police had taken the criminals to the station, the policewoman was having a chat with Irene, when they heard a panting noise and the patter of claws on the kitchen tiles. The policewoman investigated but the kitchen was empty. The WPC shook her head and looked at Irene, who had a bewildered look on her face.

"Wasn't that weird?" asked the policewoman. After finishing her tea, she left, saying that she would get someone from social services to pop in the next day to see if she needed any help and that she would send her boyfriend round to fix the broken front door. The time was now ten past four in the morning and Irene was worn out. She put two bolts on the broken door and retired to bed. At twenty to six, she was woken by something wet and cold prodding her hand, which was hanging over the bed. The wet thing was the nose of a large Alsatian, which was looking at her with brown sorrowful eyes. Irene was shocked rigid. It was her old dog Bob, who had died fourteen years ago. She reached out to stroke her faithful friend but, as she did so, the dog vanished. As the pale light of dawn came into the room, Irene was overcome by a tremendous sense of sorrow tinged with disbelief. Until that eventful morning, Irene had not believed in ghosts but now she almost cried as she realised that her dog had somehow returned from the afterlife to protect her.

There is a strange epilogue to this story: when Carla returned from France, she had some film left in her camera from the holiday trip and took a picture of her mum standing in the garden with her walking stick. When the pictures came back from the chemist, Carla exclaimed, "Hey, Mum! Look at this! There's a dog on this photo. Look, next to you in the garden."

Irene sighed when she inspected the picture. In the photograph, there was an out of focus image of a big Alsatian sitting behind her. The dog was looking at her with its head tilted. "That's Bob," Irene whispered, with a lump in her throat. She didn't want to frighten Carla, so she didn't mention the apparition of her faithful friend.

"Whose dog is it, Mum?" asked Carla.

"I'm not sure," said her mother, as a tear rolled down her cheek.

Bye Bye Baby

The following incident allegedly happened in Liverpool in 1979 and was even mentioned on local television.

In the autumn of that year, Frank Haines was driving his Ford Cortina along Queens Drive near Dunbabin Road in the Wavertree district of the city. The time was 1.45am, and it was raining heavily. Frank had been to visit his elderly mother in the Dingle and was on his way home. However, his Cortina had a troublesome engine and whenever Frank stopped at the traffic lights, the car would stall or shudder.

On this particular night, the engine died at the lights and Frank had to turn the ignition key again and again to get the car to start. Seconds before he was about to move off, a girl came splashing through the torrential rain, waving at him through the rain-lashed windscreen and then tapping on the passenger window. She looked as if she was about nineteen or twenty and wore wore a white rain-soaked tee shirt, a tartan scarf, and a pair of white flares. He leaned over and opened the door and the girl jumped in, slamming the door. She had long red hair and a pale freckled face from which she was wiping the rain. "Could you give me a lift home, mate?" she asked, smiling at Frank. "I'm drenched."

"I can see that, but do you always jump into strangers' cars like that?" asked Frank, still annoyed because the engine was refusing to start. He turned the ignition key once more and the engine fired into life. "Where do you want a lift to?" he asked the girl.

"Barnham Drive, please," said the girl and gave the number of her house.

"Where's that?" Frank asked, relieved that the car was behaving itself again.

"It's off Childwall Valley Road," said the girl, leaning back and letting out a sigh. She began singing a song Frank had not heard for years – 'Bye Bye Baby' by the Bay City Rollers.

"What're you doing out at this time?" Frank asked.

"I've been walking for the last half hour from Fir Lane through all this rain. I hate the rain, don't you?" After a short pause, she asked, "What's your name?"

"Frank. What's yours?" Frank accelerated through a set of traffic lights that were about to turn red to avoid stalling again.

"Kelly."

"Well, Kelly, you'll have to direct me to Barnham Drive."

Frank drove to the Fiveways roundabout and carried on along Childwall Valley Road.

"Thanks for the lift, Frank. Are you going out your way for me?" said Kelly, beaming at him.

"Nah, I'm not going out of the way; I live over in Court Hey. Now. Where do I go now?" said Frank, squinting at the road through the squeaking windscreen wipers.

"It's on your right here ... er, no, its the next road on the right," said Kelly. Then she tapped Frank on his left leg.

"What?" said Frank, startled.

"Frank, could you do me a big favour? But you'll think I'm cheeky," asked Kelly. "Could you wait outside the house for me, then give me a lift to my mate's in Chelwood Avenue? Could you?"

"Look, I'm not a bloody taxi driver. I'm dropping you off at your house and that's it," Frank retorted as he turned into Barnham Drive and stopped near the girl's house.

"Please, Frank? she wheedled, playfully touching his knee and pinching it, making him smile. "Pretty please?"

"Hurry up then. You've got five minutes. If this car doesn't start though, I'll have to walk home."

"Thanks, Frank. I won't be a minute. I'll just tell my dad I'm staying over at my mate's."

Kelly left the car and dashed down the road in the pouring rain. She opened her gate and disappeared behind a hedge as she ran up the path towards the front door.

Frank was thirty-three, but looked much younger and he began to wonder if he was too old to date Kelly. He soon dismissed the thought and waited for her to come back. He waited … and waited. Fifteen minutes crawled by and Frank started to get annoyed. "That's it, girl; I'm going home," he muttered to himself. He decided to give her five more minutes but she still did not return. Frank surmised that her father had told her not to get into a car with a stranger. The car started up first time and Frank began to drive off but, only a few seconds later, the car started to shake alarmingly and shuddered to a halt. Frank tried again and again to get it to restart but it just would not budge. He cursed Kelly, "Damn it! She imposed on me, now I'll ask her for help." Frank marched to Kelly's house and rang the bell, knowing deep down that it was also a good excuse to see her again. She was a very pretty girl and Frank recalled the way she had touched his leg in the car. A silhouette appeared and looked through the frosted glass. "Who is it?" said a voice behind the door.

"It's me … Frank … Is Kelly there?"

A bolt was drawn back and the handle turned. The front door opened and a man of about sixty peered out at Frank.

"Sorry to bother you, sir. Is Kelly there?" Frank asked, dripping wet and cringing with embarrassment.

"Kelly who?" the man demanded to know. He was far from friendly and it hadn't escaped Frank's notice that he was restraining an ugly looking Alsatian dog by the collar. He told the man about the red-haired girl he'd given a lift to and the man's whole demeanour changed abruptly. His pained eyes were harrowing to look at and he seemed to be carrying a terrible burden.

In halting tones he revealed that his daughter Kelly had been knocked down in a hit and run incident on Fir Lane four years ago. He was so shaken by what Frank had told him that he invited him in out of the rain and showed him his photo album of Kelly. In one photograph, she was dressed in the tartan and white flares that Bay City Rollers fans wore and Frank remembered the song she had sung in his car – 'Bye Bye Baby'. Just before Kelly died, her friend in Court Hey had had an argument with her and cried her eyes out when she heard that Kelly had died. She kept saying she wished she could tell Kelly she was sorry.

It is said that Kelly's ghost still walks up Fir Lane and has even been seen by the police. In 1990, it was reported that a Royal Mail van swerved to avoid the ghost of a red-haired girl who vanished in the middle of the road.

YOU'RE DEAD!

The Bullring is a row of tenements off Brownlow Hill, so-called because of their circular layout. In 1972, at a flat in these tenements, a paranormal incident occurred, which was witnessed by four people, including two policemen.

A young couple, Julie and Frank, moved into a flat on the top floor of the Bullring in the summer of 1972. Julie was a barmaid at a local pub, the Oxford, and Frank worked at a bakery in Toxteth. One night, at around 11 o'clock, Frank returned home from the bakery and saw that Julie was not yet home. He was about to cook himself a readymeal, and listen to some music when he heard a dreadful noise next door. "Noisy neighbours. That's all I need right now," Frank tutted.

The noise got steadily worse and Frank heard the man next door shout, "You idiot! You've really done it now!"

Then a woman's hysterical voice screamed, "I'm sorry, Keith!" Followed by the sound of objects being thrown and plates being smashed.

Frank thumped on the wall and shouted, "Oi! That's enough! Shut up!"

The noise subsided for a while, but half an hour later, when Frank was settling down to eat his supper, the squabbling began again.

"I can't believe what you've done. That's it, you're dead now, girl, you're dead!" shouted the man.

"No, you're dead now! I mean it!" she screamed back.

More plates were smashing as there came a knock at the door. Frank got up, accidentally tipping the plate with his supper on to the sofa. His blood was boiling as he answered the door to let Julie in. She hurried inside, telling him that two policemen were on the landing, hammering on next door because there was a domestic taking place. "Tell me about it," said Frank. "They're at each other's throats."

The screams next door got louder, so the policemen had no choice but to kick the door in. Inside, they found no one, just fragments of crockery in the kitchen and smashed ornaments in the living room. They looked out of the window, just in case the battling couple had jumped or pushed each other to the street below, but they had not.

Three hours later, the grim truth came out. The couple could not have been having a heated argument because they were dead. They had died earlier that evening in a car crash over a mile away in Princes Road. The woman, who had been driving, had been drinking and had hit a lamppost at 50mph, killing herself and her husband instantly.

When one of their relatives turned up at the flat and spoke to Frank and Julie about the tragedy, Frank's blood ran cold as he remembered what he had heard the man next door saying: "I can't believe what you've done. That's it, you're dead now!" and she had replied, "No! you're dead!" It suddenly all made sense to Frank. He had heard the two spirits of the crash victims arguing over who was to blame for their untimely deaths.

THE CHRISTMAS SPECTRE

There is a certain old house in Liverpool's Clarence Street that is the scene of supernatural unrest every time the festive season is upon us. Strange rappings are heard on doors and the sounds of a disgruntled voice cursing a long-dead man named Charles reach their height around Christmas Eve, when the ghost puts in an appearance. He is about fifty who wears a long purple velveteen coat, a grey waistcoat and a pair of long narrow trousers. Many people have seen him over the years, from the late nineteenth century to the present day. From the accounts given by witnesses, we know that the Christmas spectre smokes an ectoplasmic pipe and wears a pair of wire-framed spectacles, over which he peers as he paces back and forth before a cast-iron fireplace in the sitting room of the house.

The phantom goes through his paces in his personal limbo at the same time every Christmas Eve, at precisely ten to eleven at night and invariably ends his ghostly performance by resting his head on the mantelpiece and sobbing. He then fades away, leaving an aromatic mist of pipe tobacco hanging in the air.

Five years ago, the ghost put in his usual seasonal appearance and the poor tomcat of the family who were staying there was so startled that it leapt out of a first floor window, almost ending life number nine.

Generations of residents have pondered on the ghost's identity, but a couple of years ago, a certain professional ghost researcher and two local historians finally solved the mystery of this ghost of Christmas past and here is the tale they uncovered.

At the aforementioned address in Clarence Street, there lived a middle-aged bachelor, a doctor named Humphrey Brooke, who became infatuated with a girl less than half his age – the daughter of a Duke Street shipping magnate – Felicia Clayton. Felicia was twenty years old with flaxen hair and a stunningly curvaceous figure. Many men were in love with her and she was constantly receiving invitations to every ball and soiree in the city. Humphrey Brooke, on the other hand, was around fifty years old and knew that he would never be regarded as attractive by the opposite sex. He had a hook nose, failing eyesight, a stoop from hunching over his medical books and a wheezy cough brought on by his incessant pipe-smoking. As if that weren't enough, he suffered crippling bouts of rheumatism in his joints. Yet, he was completely infatuated with the seemingly untouchable Felicia.

It all began when Brooke attended the funeral of Jesse Hartley, the eminent engineer who had transformed the Liverpool waterfront with his magnificent docks and warehouses. Felicia and her father attended the funeral too, and Dr Brooke was briefly introduced to the young beauty. He kissed her hand and she smiled at him several times during that sombre afternoon. Since that glorious afternoon, he had only seen Miss Clayton twice; once in Rodney

Street, alighting from a hansom cab and, on the second occasion, she had waved to him in Bold Street while walking hand in hand with a rich suitor, a young Colonel Burns. The way charming way in which Felicia had acknowledged him, with that wave of her gloved hand, took his breath away. The girl and her beau walked on down Bold Street but she turned twice and smiled at Dr Brooke, which turned the Colonel crimson with jealousy.

The bachelor Brooke returned to his house with a new spring in his step and wrote of his encounters with Felicia in a little black book. He also scribbled down his outrageous plans to win Felicia's heart. The most realistic plan was quite straightforward. A Christmas Eve ball was to take place at the prestigious address of a Rodney Street magistrate. Humphrey Brooke had already received an invitation and the invitation card stated that the doctor was entitled to bring a lady friend. accordingly, Mr Brooke lovingly wrote the name Felicia Clayton on the invitation and dreamily studied how the ornate card looked with his name next to that of the light of his life.

The following morning, Dr Brooke's friend, Charles Wilson, the proprietor of a corn mill, visited his friend at the surgery in Clarence Street. Wilson was five years younger than him and enjoyed a legendary reputation for being a womaniser. He asked Brooke if he had anything planned for Christmas and asked him if he wanted a bit of company in the taverns of Liverpool over the festive season. Dr Brooke surprised him by saying that he had plans for Christmas Eve which involved a beautiful young woman. "This isn't another of your fantasies involving a certain Miss Clayton, who is young enough to be your daughter, is it?" laughed Clayon, rather cruelly.

Before he could think of a suitable riposte, a woman

rushed into the surgery and pleaded with Dr Brooke to come at once to treat her father, who had collapsed with a seizure. Brooke knew the woman's father well, so he grabbed his medical bag and rushed out of the surgery, leaving Wilson behind. Wilson was a nosey fellow and he opened a drawer in the doctor's desk and pulled out the little black book. He grinned and sniggered as he read the book's entries concerning Felicia.

"Ah, there's no fool like an old fool," Wilson whispered to himself, as he noticed the invitation card with his friend's name on, and Felicia's name next to it.

Wilson was intrigued by his friend's crush on the sensuous, young woman and paid a visit to Dr Brooke the following afternoon. Wilson chuckled and slyly asked the doctor if Felicia had accepted his invitation. Brooke was outraged, realising that Wilson had read his secret journal. "How dare you pry into my personal life?" said Brooke, deeply offended. But the lovelorn doctor had a surprise for his nosey friend. He produced a letter and handed it to him.

"What's this? A writ for prying?" Wilson joked, but when he read the letter, its contents wiped the smile off his face. It was from Felicia Clayton. She had accepted Dr Brooke's invitation to the ball and Wilson was instantly consumed with jealousy. He threw the letter on the desk and flounced out, saying, "Ha! It will all come to nothing. Age and youth are like oil and water, they can never mix."

That Christmas Eve, Doctor Brooke wore a fine purple velveteen jacket and his best embroidered grey silken waistcoat. He stood before the fireplace, pacing up and down, with butterflies in his stomach, a feeling he had not experienced since the courting days of his youth, so many years ago. Then came a heavy jangling of the front door bell, which startled the doctor. He answered, thinking that perhaps Felicia had decided to call upon him, but the caller was a shivering red-nosed youth; a messenger boy, who handed Dr Brooke a sealed envelope. Brooke tipped the messenger and read the letter. His heart broke on the spot. Felicia had undergone a change of heart and no longer wished to go to the dance with the doctor. She would now be going with her long-time admirer, Colonel Burns. The curt letter, written by Felicia's stern father, warned Brooke to keep away from his daughter and to act his age. Unbeknown to Brooke, his so-called friend Charles Wilson had sent an anonymous letter to Felicia's father, warning him of Dr Brooke's 'outrageous and obnoxious plans to have romantic involvements' with Felicia.

Felicia, however, was a strong-headed girl and disobeyed her father's instructions by looking everywhere for Dr Brooke at the ball. She knew he was not much to look at, but his romantic letters had moved her, and Felicia had been determined to meet him. When he failed to turn up, Felicia went home, much to the disappointment of all the men at the ball.

Meanwhile the letter had left Dr Brooke feeling bereft and, on that Christmas Eve, he died from what seems to have been a heart attack, brought on by the emotional turmoil of Felicia's apparent rejection. Brooke knocked off the clock from the mantelpiece as he fell dead on the hearth rug. The clock broke; its dial recording that his death had occurred at precisely ten to eleven.

THE DEVIL'S CHILDREN

The following chilling story took place in the North-West in November, 1858. Isaac West, a writer from Wolverhampton, was travelling around the country collecting folk tales for a book. He was determined to spend as many years as necessary visiting every corner of Britain, in order to record every tale and myth in the land. He did not believe in ghosts, or the world of the supernatural, and thought that the Devil was just a figment of the human imagination.

On this particular foggy evening, West mounted his horse and rode from a country inn on the outskirts of Ormskirk towards a lodging house near the town of Rufford, just five miles to the north. During the journey he noticed a rosy glow in the forest to his left. Curiosity got the better of him and he dismounted, tethered the reins of his horse to a tree and set off towards the light. As he drew nearer he realised that it was a bonfire, around which thirty robed figures were standing in a circle, all wearing pointed white hats with eye-holes cut out. This was ten years before the Ku Klux Klan was founded, but the costumes bore an uncanny resemblance to those which were later worn by members of the racist secret society in America.

As he crept closer to get a better view, West saw one of the figures take a crying baby from a box and walk over to the fire, while the other figures chanted. West noticed that there was an enormous wooden cross with a man crucified upon it above the raging flames, and that it was a real body on the cross and not an effigy. The cross was turned upside down and so was the figure on it. The bonfire had been built around this horrific crucifixion and the man on the cross looked burnt to charcoal. The figure cradling the child moved even nearer to the fire. West was horrified. It seemed as if the figure was about to throw the baby on to the flames. He knew it was suicidal but something inside him impelled him to try and save the baby. Snapping off a large leafless branch, he saw that the figure was now holding the baby up to the burnt man on the upside-down cross. West rushed up to the back of him, whacking him hard on the back of the head with the heavy branch. The other startled figures watched, immobile, as he grabbed the baby from the masked sadist and dash back into the forest.

Isaac West careered through the forest with the baby in his arms, with the masked figures hot on his heels. He felt a stabbing stitch of pain in his side but kept on running. Because of the fog, he had lost track of where he had tied up his horse and he feared for his life, because he knew those people in close pursuit were Devil worshippers and would think nothing of killing him.

Then, mercifully, the outline of his horse appeared out of the fog and West raced towards it but, as he did so, a rifle shot whistled past his head and the horse whinnied pitifully and fell down. West kept running, although he felt his lungs were going to explode. He thought about dropping the child and running off to save his own life but just could not bring himself to commit such a cowardly act. Emerging out of the forest, he prayed for God's intervention. Just then the lamps of a stagecoach appeared further down the road, near the village of Parbold. As the clatter of the coach horses drew nearer, West ran into the road and attempted to flag it down. He frantically waved at the driver, and glanced to see the hooded figures watching from the forest.

The coach pulled up and West fell to his knees with gratitude and exhaustion, still clutching the crying baby.

"What in damnation is going on?" came a distinguished

voice from inside the coach. Isaac West instantly recognised that rich deep voice; it belonged to Horace Jones, a rich industrialist and patron to the arts. West knew him well. He had been a dinner guest of Horace and his Mawdesley-born wife at their magnificent mansion near Nantwich on many occasions over the years. Just what Horace was doing so far north in the dead of night was a mystery but West was so relieved to hear his voice that he gave it little thought.

Horace looked out of the window and squinted at the man holding the baby, "Is that you, Isaac?"

"Horace!" gasped West, pointing to the forest and describing what lurked within its shadowy depths. The magnate seemed very nervous about what he was hearing and, as West made a grab for the doorhandle of the coach, shouted, "No! Stay there! Wait a moment!"

West pleaded with him, saying the baby was going to die of pneumonia in the freezing night air and impatiently pulled open the carriage door, in time to see Horace hurriedly taking off the same weird robes that the Devil worshippers had worn in the forest. On the seat next to Horace Jones was a pointed hat with the distinctive eye holes, just like the ones the Devil worshippers were wearing. West was stunned and needed a few seconds to digest what he had seen. Seeing that he had been found out, the industrialist reached into his inside pocket but West dived at him, punching him in the face and making his nose bleed. He then grabbed a small pistol from Horace's inside jacket pocket and held it against his forehead. "Tell the coachman to take us from this accursed place, or I will not hesitate to blow your brains out!" demanded West.

Horace saw the mad look in West's eyes and screamed to the coachman, "Do as he says! Hurry, man!" As the coach thundered towards the village of Shevington, Horace claimed that he had been going to attend the sacrifice in the woods in order to infiltrate the group and spy upon the satanists. West refused to believe him and quizzed him about the infant. Horace said it was probably from some girl who was herself a satanist.

After leaving the baby in the care of a landlord of a tavern in Shevington, West reported Horace to the sheriff. But Horace was rich and powerful and quickly bought himself out of his unsavoury predicament. He claimed that West had an over-imaginative mind but when West and several policemen revisited the spot in the forest, they all found the remains of the bonfire and the blackened upturned cross with its corpse. It was determined that the body on that cross was not alive when it had been cremated, but had been dug up from the local cemetery before being nailed to the cross. Despite the overwhelming evidence – including the remains of his dead horse, West was strongly advised, by certain people in high-ranking positions whom he could not name, to leave the area and go back to Wolverhampton.

It later came to light that there was a satanic cult calling themselves 'The Devil's Children' at work in the area committing rape and murder.

LAST DANCE

There is a church in Liverpool's Edge Hill district that was once the setting of a tragic romance. The man and woman in this long-forgotten drama were Olivia Stroud, a beautiful porcelain-skinned girl of twenty-one, and her childhood sweetheart James Divine, a soldier. Olivia and James were both born in Marmaduke Street within days of each other in 1899. They lived next door to each other and were the best of friends. At fourteen, they had both fallen in love and vowed to marry one day. Sadly, the First World War intervened and James returned from the infamous Battle of the Somme a changed man. His grim experiences of the futile carnage had turned him to drink and transformed him into a sarcastic troublemaker. Yet Olivia knew that in James' troubled soul there were traces of the boy she loved so well.

In 1920, a dance was held at the church in Durning Road and James turned up with a few of his old comrades from the war. Several times, Olivia asked him to dance with her but James always replied, "No, I'll join you at the last dance," and continued drinking with his friends.

Olivia's beauty was legendary in the district and she was known as 'The Belle of Edge Hill'. Today, Olivia would undoubtedly have been snapped up by the film industry. She was not only extraordinarily attractive but was also full of charisma. All the young men sighed as she took to the floor with an elderly man who had dared to ask her to dance, but James just stood at the makeshift bar with a sarcastic look on his face as Olivia waltzed by.

By midnight, James was fairly intoxicated and the sentimental boy Olivia once knew started to show through the soldier's tough but false front. As he watched her walk towards him, his heart burned with sorrow. He should have danced with her earlier, instead of humouring his mates. Something deep down told him that there would never be another night like this and he reached out to his childhood sweetheart as a crowd of jealous men looked on. Suddenly, Olivia stopped smiling and stood still. She bowed her head and looked drowsy.

"Olivia ... what's wrong?" said James rushing over to her.

Olivia seemed dizzy and fell down on to the wooden panelled floor of the church hall, as the colour started to drain from her beautiful face. "James, I don't feel well. Take me home."

"Olivia! Somebody please get a doctor," he cried.

He lifted her in his arms but did not know what to do. An old grey-haired man rushed from the crowd and said he was a doctor. He told James to lay her on the floor where he took her pulse, then felt her forehead. The doctor diagnosed that she had a fever of some sort. She was taken home to Marmaduke Street and became delirious. She kept saying, "James, what about the last dance? Why wouldn't you dance with me?"

At one in the morning, Olivia stopped breathing and quietly died with James at her side. He cried unashamedly over the body of his first and last love.

The postmortem revealed that Olivia had been poisoned in a most bizarre way. The girl's parents had recently fallen on hard times and had bought a secondhand dress from a tailor in London Road for her to wear to the dance. The tailor had obtained the dress from an undertaker who later confessed that he had stolen it from the body of a girl prior to her burial. That girl had been embalmed, and the dress had soaked up a quantity of the poisonous embalming fluid. The fluid had seeped out of the dress and through the pores of Olivia's skin as she danced, slowly poisoning her. After her death, James drove himself insane with self reproach and drank himself into an early grave.

In 1942, an ARP warden patrolling Edge Hill during a blackout, spotted a faint light coming from a church. On entering the church, he saw that the light was radiating from the ghostly figure of a young woman in a white dress who was walking across the hall with her head bowed.

Even today, the ghost of the tragic Olivia is still seen, walking across the church hall, waiting in vain for that last dance with her long-dead sweetheart.

THE TRUTH WILL OUT

According to an old Irish proverb, 'A guilty conscience needs no accuser,' and the following true story is about the conscience of a killer's mind. It is also said that a criminal always returns to the scene of his crime.

In the year 1855, Henry Arkle, a forty-year-old timber merchant, bumped into Charles Wilson, a window cleaner, in Liverpool's Dale Street. Arkle had lent the window cleaner money five months previously to pay off a gambling debt and Wilson still had not paid a farthing of it back to the merchant. Arkle grabbed the window cleaner by his lapels and shook him, "You'll pay up some of the money you owe me. Right now!" Wilson promised to do so on the following Friday when he had collected his wages and explained that he had not been feeling well recently because he had been suffering from food poisoning. Friday came and went but Charlie Wilson did not pay his debt.

At that time, in Liverpool, the poor had been rioting after a disastrous harvest and flour and wheat were being sold at a premium. Shops and bakeries were plundered by the hungry mob and Henry Arkle got caught up in the middle of one of these riots and came across Charlie Wilson hurling a coping-stone through a baker's window. Arkle pulled down his hat till it covered his eyes and pushed through the crowd. When he was behind Wilson, who was urging the rioters to steal the bread, he reached into his boot and pulled out a short dagger called a dirk, which had been given to him by his Scottish uncle. He glanced furtively around and seeing that the rioters were too preoccupied to notice, plunged the dagger into Wilson's back. He stabbed him repeatedly as he cheered on the rioters in the deafening din. Wilson turned around slowly, spluttering up blood from his punctured lungs. He had the terrible expression of a man who knows he is about to die as he looked Arkle in the eye and asked, "Why?"

Henry Arkle suddenly burned with guilt, and shoved the stabbed window cleaner to the ground, where he was trampled by the mob as they rushed towards the bakery. The police made enquiries but Charles Wilson's killer could not be found, so they surmised that he had accidentally been killed by the mob.

A month later, at midnight, an old woman called at Arkle's house off Mount Pleasant claiming she had seen him knife Wilson during the riot. She demanded one hundred pounds or she would go straight to the police. Should he try to harm her, she confidently promised that her husband would go straight to the police. Henry Arkle had an excellent memory and knew that she was just a poor match-seller who lived on her own in Roscoe Street. He had seen her many times and knew she had no husband. Pretending to go and fetch the blackmailer her money, he picked up his dagger instead, and cut her throat.

He locked his doors and decapitated the woman with a hacksaw, planning to throw the unidentifiable and headless body into the Liverpool to Leeds canal. He stoked the fire, then placed the old woman's head on it. The grey hair singed and quickly ignited and the flames turned the flesh black. The stench was sick making and the heat had a strange effect on the head, causing the eyelids to shoot open. The eyes looked out at the horrified merchant with an accusing stare. Arkle screamed out and thrust the glowing poker into one of the eyeballs and it popped, showering him with a vile watery fluid.

At 3am, the merchant carted the headless naked body of

the old woman to the Liverpool and Leeds canal near Vauxhall Road and dumped it in. It was tied to three heavy stones, so sank to the bottom with a loud splash. Arkle watched as the ripples radiated across the waters of the canal, as the body submerged. Back home, Henry turned his attention to the one-eyed head of the blackmailer. It just would not burn, so he buried it in the small garden in front of his house beneath the rockery.

The double murderer finally got to bed around 5am., but shortly after falling asleep, the dreams began. He dreamt of the old woman's head on the fire and when her eyes would open he would awake with a scream. Another distressing dream pricked at his conscience. He felt himself rising up out of his bed and, after floating out of the window, he would fly across the rooftops until he was hovering over the moonlit cemetery in Church Alley, off Church Street. Then he would start to descend towards a pauper's grave with a little stone marker at its head. He knew this grave all too well. It was that of the window cleaner and he had visited that grave many times out of guilt and to pray for forgiveness. In the nightmare, Arkle would descend through the cold clay until he was in the coffin with his victim. The dream ended with the murder victim saying, "I'm still alive. Please dig me up, Henry! I'm still alive!" and Charlie Wilson would then start to scream and scratch at the coffin lid until his fingernails were shredded and dripping with blood. He would become hysterical and smash his forehead against the coffin lid, as he tried in vain to get out the claustrophobic box. Henry Arkle woke up at this point, soaked in sweat, his heart pounding in his ears.

These unbearable nightmares haunted Henry Arkle for weeks. The merchant's business suffered, and he slowly descended into insanity bankruptcy. One morning, he caused a commotion by screaming at a group of pigeons in his front garden, thinking they were pecking at the remains of the old woman's head but they were just pecking at a small millet plant that had sprung up in the rockery. The neighbours sneered at him as they watched him constantly peeping out at the front garden with a look of dread.

That autumn, Henry Arkle's conscience finally got the better of his warped mind. At three in the morning, he left his house with a spade and lantern wrapped in a sack. He was pale and had black rings around his bloodshot eyes – having not enjoyed a good night's sleep in months because of all the nightmares. He sneaked down the back streets until he reached the shadows of a church which stood on the site now occupied by a clothing shop in Church Street. Arkle scaled the cemetery railings and lighting his lantern, roamed the gravestones until he found the pauper's grave where Charles Wilson had been laid to rest. In Arkle's twisted mind, Wilson was still alive and if he could be dug up, the world would see that he was not a murderer.

They say a madman has extra strength and Arkle frantically spaded away like a machine. Not once did he stop and at last his spade hit the lid of the coffin. He sighed, "It won't be long now, Mr Wilson," and started to smash the lid of the cheaply made coffin to splinters with the spade. The racket alerted a policeman who was patrolling nearby. Climbing over the cemetery gates, he noticed the lantern by edge of the open grave. Peering down, he saw Henry Arkle shaking the rotting body of his murder victim. Worms wriggled out of the corpse's eye sockets and teeth as Arkle screamed, "No! You're not dead! You told me to dig you up! You can't be dead!"

The policeman blew hard on his whistle and alerted his colleagues. Arkle was taken to the bridewell in Cheapside and made a full confession. After taking the statements from him, the recording officer told everyone to get some sleep, as a proper hearing would resume in the morning. Arkle was put in his cell but, as usual, did not sleep a wink … and probably never did until he was hanged from the end of a rope a month later.

THE LEGEND OF MARY CRANE

There is an old proverb, 'Speak of the Devil and he'll appear'. That saying is a throwback to an old belief in the power of spoken magic or spells, as we call them.

This final tale concerns a witch who was greatly feared by her community in the picturesque setting of the Forest of Bowland. Even today, the mere mention of the Witch of Bowland Forest is greeted with an uneasy silence in a certain Lancashire tavern. An old legend says that the eyes of her corpse will fly open in her grave if her name is so much as uttered …

In December 1812, three woodcutters from the village of Abbeystead, which lies seven miles south-east of Lancaster, were instructed by Lord Trenchard to bring an enormous fir tree from the Forest of Bowland. He had personally selected the tree and chalked a white cross upon its bark. The woodcutters were to chop the tree down and cart it back to Abbeystead. It seemed a simple enough task, but the woodcutters reached the forest only after making a detour to an old friend who made his own cider, and by the time they reached the forest they were quite drunk. One waved a hatchet and the other two carried a long saw and they sang as they rolled along the path into the dense forest.

The oldest woodcutter, a well-built man named John Perry, spotted the white cross on the huge fir tree and saw to his dismay that it was almost forty feet in height. That meant that the men would have to haul the tree on to the cart and have it drawn back to the village by their two old shire horses – a daunting task. The three men set about sawing through the fir's hard trunk but it was very thirsty work. Perry told his workmates, two young twins, Norman and Daniel, to have a go at sawing , but they too found the task demanding. After a while, young Norman pointed to a clearing, "Look. Someone lives there. They might spare us a drink and some food."

A quaint-looking little wooden house was half hidden behind some trees. It was crudely built, little more than a shanty. When a young woman in her twenties, with long black hair, emerged from the hut carrying a basket, the three men smiled and, as she passed by, old Mr Perry tipped his hat, "Good day to ye, Miss." But the woman just looked the men up and down and walked on. She went over to the base of a tree, picked some toadstools, put them in her basket and wandered off into the forest. When she was out of sight, Mr Perry said, "My, she was a pretty maiden. Let us see if her family's at home."

They went over to the hut and peeped through the window. There was no sign of anybody inside, so the men pulled open the door and entered. They soon realised that they had entered the home of a witch. A small cauldron hung on a chain over a flickering fire and, on the hearth-stone near the grate, was a human skull, probably unearthed from Abbeystead graveyard. Hanging from one of the crossbeams of the low ceiling was a collection of little effigies made from rags and real human hair with pins stuck in them.

One of the twins picked up a book and flipped through its pages. There were detailed drawings of plants with notes scribbled under the diagrams. Then Perry noticed a small round table with a black cloth upon it. Picking up the cloth, he revealed a large egg-shaped piece of polished amber.

"What the deuce is that?" asked one of the twins.

"Some type of crystal ball, I imagine," replied Perry.

Suddenly, they recoiled in fright as the faint image of a blue eye appeared in the amber and stared back at them. The three ran out of the house in terror. After they had recovered from the shock, Perry remarked, "It must be the house of Mary Crane." The mere mention of the name made them all shiver. What happened next is not too clear, but Mary Crane saw the men coming from her house as she returned from the forest. She dropped her basket and raised her hands to the men, as if she was about to cast some evil spell on them. Daniel ran off in a state of terror and did not stop until he reached the village of Abbeystead.

He returned to the clearing with a mob but there was no sign of Mary Crane, nor Mr Perry, nor his brother Norman. Then, one of the villagers pointed to the fir tree marked with a cross. There, nailed to its trunk, were the bodies of old Mr Perry and Norman. The men had been nailed to the tree with long iron spikes that penetrated their foreheads and necks.

The vicar of Abbeystead, stirred up the mob by crying out, "See what this agent of the Devil has done! Mary Crane will be hanged for this crime, for it is written in the scriptures, 'Thou shalt not suffer a witch to live!' Find her and kill her!"

A strange twilight fell on the forest and the temperature plummeted until the cold was unbearable. The mob hurried back along the road to Abbeystead and, during their retreat, the sound of a woman cackling could be heard nearby. And a large black cat leapt out of a tree and attacked the vicar. The overgrown feline seized his head and clawed one of his eyes out of its socket. The mob, in a panic, stampeded back to the village.

The following morning, just after sunrise, a larger mob returned to the little wooden house of Mary Crane and tried to set fire to it with torches and buckets of tar, yet the wooden dwelling refused to burn. The mob resorted to smashing up the house with hatchets, then returned to the village. That night, the beer in the tavern turned sour and several farm animals dropped dead for no apparent reason. At the first stroke of midnight, the barmaid at the tavern screamed and clutched at her face. The red, blistering imprint of a hand slowly appeared on her cheek and the impression never went away. She was scarred for life.

On Christmas Eve, two travellers from Lancaster came down a country road to Abbeystead to visit their relatives for Christmas and observed a crowd of people dressed in white walking in the moonlight on the edge of Bowland Forest. One of the travellers thought the figures were ghosts and wanted to ride away but his companion persuaded him to take a closer look at the nocturnal activity. They rode into the forest and what they saw made them shiver. The people were wearing nightgowns and nightdresses and seemed to be in a trance. It was almost as if they were all sleepwalking. But these sleepwalkers were carrying out tasks under the supervision of a young woman dressed in black. As the fascinated travellers came nearer to the bizarre scene, they recognised four of their own relatives among the fifty-odd crowd. The group was building a new home for the woman on the other side of the forest and the travellers realised that the weird taskmaster was none other than Mary Crane. One of the travellers produced a pistol and fired at the witch and she shrieked, running off into the forest, followed by a large black cat. At that precise moment, all the somnambulists awoke from their trance and were puzzled to find themselves in the forest. The last thing they remembered was going to bed.

The villagers requested the services of a professional witch-hunter and some six months later, an old man rode into Abbeystead. His name was George Mandeville and he convinced Lord Trenchard that he had the skill to rid the terrified villagers of the witch. He used a dowsing rod to track her down and he and a group of armed villagers encircled Mary Crane with salt and captured her.

She was hanged the same day and Mandeville had her buried face-down beneath a certain crossroads near the village. He then ordered the villagers never to even breathe one mention of her name, warning that each mention of Mary Crane would give her spirit more and more strength to return to life with a vengeance. The villagers obeyed Mandeville's advice, but one particular villager wrote the story down and committed it to posterity. So now that you have read this story, please do not repeat it and talk of you-know-who; or she may just pay you a visit.

A LABOUR OF LUST

The following tale allegedly occurred in the small village of Ambleford, near Gresford, in Cheshire. Sadly, the village no longer exists, but records show that Ambleford was a very prosperous and close-knit community.

One warm summer evening in 1740, Becky, a beautiful gypsy girl, was waiting in a meadow outside the village for her boyfriend Robin, a blacksmith's son. The eighteen year-old was a real beauty and turned the heads of every man in the village. Yet she only had eyes for Robin, who was just fifteen. Robin's father was a drunken bully who banned his son from seeing any gypsy girls, but Robin still met Becky in secret whenever he could and intended to run away with her to be married at Gretna Green.

On this particular summer night, a huge full moon loomed over the countryside and the gypsy girl felt there was something evil afoot. She waited for Robin for ages but he was nowhere to be seen. He had been caught sneaking out of his bedroom window and had received a hiding with the strap from his father.

At around one in the morning, just as a barn owl hooted, a sinister figure came out of the nearby woods and approached the gypsy girl. He was just a shadow because his back was turned to the moon. The figure called out, "Becky, come hither, girl." The voice sounded vaguely familiar, so Becky walked over to the man and saw that he wore a highwayman's mask, but by then it was too late. He pounced on her as she turned to run but tripped over her flowing skirts. Within a heartbeat, the man was on top of her. He pinned her down with his muscular arms and forced kisses on her face, neck and breasts. Becky tried to scream but the man hit her across the face three times and produced a small flintlock pistol. He pressed the barrel against the frightened girl's bosom and whispered, "If you cry out, I'll shoot you through the heart."

Becky quivered with fear as the attacker dug the barrel hard against her breast and gritted his teeth. The man then pulled up her dress and what followed was a cowardly sexual assault. The man then got to his feet, pulled up his trousers and ran off into the moonlit woods. Becky just lay there on the floor, sobbing.

Becky never told Robin about the attack. However, she did go to her old gypsy grandmother, a woman named Ursula, and told her about the rape. Ursula dangled a strange-looking pendulum over Becky's abdomen then muttered a spell. She then smiled and said, "You will bear no child. No seed has taken root." Becky started cried with relief and held her grandmother's hand. Ursula suddenly started murmuring what seemed to be the words of a hex and she seemed very angry as she cast the spell. Then the old woman explained what her magic would do. "Do you know what couvade is, girl?"

Becky shook her head. She was not yet well versed in the occult lore of the Romany people.

Old Ursula explained, "Sometimes a man goes through labour pains when his wife is suffering in her pregnancy. That is known as couvade. It only happens when the man has been lustful. If a man who loves his wife dearly impregnates her, he suffers no such pains. I tell you truly Becky, the man who ravished you shall have labour pains as if he were giving birth to the Devil."

Becky was intrigued by her grandmother's words. The months went by, and Robin and Becky courted through the autumn and winter. Finally, Robin proposed and offered her a simple golden ring. Becky said she loved him but told him that she thought they were too young to marry. Robin insisted that he was old enough and pleaded for her to say yes but the girl was not sure. Robin then suggested running away to Gretna Green but neither of them had any money, so they walked along the lonely country lane in the snow, holding hands and feeling depressed. Suddenly, they saw a riderless horse wandering around further up the lane in a clearing. On the ground was a man who looked as if he was dying. Robin instantly recognised him as the vicar of

Ambleford, the Reverend Morley. Robin and Becky ran up to him and asked what ailed him.

"Help me, I feel as if I've been poisoned!" said the Reverend, and he curled up and squirmed in the dust.

Robin bent down and saw something very strange. The Reverend – who was a rather thin man – had a round bulging belly. This round mass actually seemed to contract in and out as as if it had a life of its own. Becky recognised the voice of her attacker and realised that it had been the Reverend Morley who had molested her on that moonlit nightand now he was suffering the labour pains of childbirth, thanks to Ursula's spell.

When Morley set eyes on the gypsy girl, he had guilt written all over his face, and he cried, "You've had a curse of couvade put upon me, wench. I beg you to break this spell! Please. Here! Have all my money!"

The reverend took out his full purse and threw it at Becky. The girl took it and pulled Robin away by the arm and explained what Morley had done. Robin was so furious that he wanted to harm the priest but Becky simply said, "Let him suffer, that's enough," and the couple left Ambleford with the money and went to be married at Gretna Green.

They settled in Carlisle and life was good. They prospered and had many children. Then, one day, out of curiosity, Robin returned to Ambleford in disguise. He asked the new vicar what had become of Morley and he told a very interesting tale. He said that Morley's stomach had swollen up to such an extent that he had become stuck between the gateposts of his house. Several people struggled to free him but the agony was too much and in the end he confessed to the rape of the gypsy girl. The authorities accused him of murdering the couple, who had not been seen for years, and imprisoned him. However, before the trial could begin, the vicar was found dead on the floor of his cell. He was surrounded by a pool of blood and water and the strange bulge in his stomach had gone. One of the guards noticed something very peculiar – tiny footprints of blood leading away from the body. These footprints were doubly strange because they only had three toes!

"There was a lot of talk about it in the village," said the vicar, "and some said it looked as if the evil Reverend Morley had given birth to a little devil …"

If you have had a paranormal encounter, or a supernatural experience of any sort, please drop a line to Tom Slemen c/o the address below.

THE BLUECOAT PRESS
3 Brick Street
Liverpool L1 0BL

Telephone 0151 707 2390
Website www.bluecoatpress.co.uk